Wok cookbook for beginners

250 Flavor-Packed Recipes to Stir-Fry, Steam, and Savor at Home

Clara Lion

Table of Contents

Introduction

Why This Book is For You

Embark on a journey of culinary exploration with "Wok Cookbook for Beginners". This book is not just about recipes; it's a comprehensive guide that transforms your kitchen into an adventure-filled hub of flavors. It's crafted for you, the modern woman, who is eager to dive into the art of wok cooking, blending nourishment with creativity. Picture yourself after a hectic day, turning to your wok instead of the takeout menu, and being enveloped in the sizzle and aroma of fresh ingredients. This book simplifies complex Asian flavors and techniques, making the wok not just a tool, but a canvas for your culinary creations.

Impress and Express: Diverse Recipes for Every Occasion

"Diverse Recipes for Every Occasion" within "Wok Cookbook for Beginners" offers an array of dishes that will not only diversify your cooking skills but also leave your friends and family in awe. From intimate family dinners to dazzling social gatherings, these recipes are designed to impress. You'll discover dishes that could grace the tables of fine dining establishments, yet they're simplified for your kitchen. This section of the book is about those moments of pride and joy when your culinary creations become the center of attention.

A Culinary Adventure in Your Hands

"A Culinary Adventure in Your Hands" is the essence of "Wok Cookbook for Beginners". This book is more than a collection of recipes; it's a lifestyle shift. It empowers you to take control of your diet, understand your ingredients, and revel in the joy of cooking. It's about transforming your kitchen experiences from routine to remarkable, ensuring that each meal is an opportunity for celebration and exploration. Through these pages, you will not just learn to cook; you will learn to celebrate food, life, and the joy of creating something extraordinary with your own hands.

In "Wok Cookbook for Beginners", you're not just acquiring a book; you're unlocking a world where cooking is a delightful journey of tastes and aromas. This book is for the dreamer, the doer, the creator in you – ready to explore the wonders of wok cooking, one delicious dish at a time.

How to Use This Cookbook

Embracing the Wok: Your Culinary Companion

Welcome to "Wok Cookbook for Beginners," a guide that transforms the humble wok into your most cherished kitchen ally. This book isn't just about following recipes; it's about embarking on a culinary journey. Approach it not just as a reader, but as an explorer. Begin with the Introduction, immersing yourself in the world of wok cooking. Understand its cultural significance, its versatility, and how it can revolutionize your everyday meals.

Navigating Your Culinary Path

Delve into Chapter I, "Wok Basics," to build a solid foundation. Here, you will learn about the wok's rich history, discover how to choose the right wok for your kitchen, and explore essential tools for wok cooking. This chapter is crucial – understanding your wok is the first step towards mastering it. Pay special attention to the sections on seasoning and caring for your wok, as these practices will enhance your cooking experience and extend the life of your wok.

From Quick Dishes to Gourmet Delights

Chapters II through VII offer a variety of recipes and techniques, from quick, easy dishes to elaborate, gourmet meals. Whether you're pressed for time on a busy weeknight or planning a leisurely weekend feast, these chapters cater to every schedule and culinary inclination. In "Quick Start Guide," you'll find recipes that are perfect for those nights when time is of the essence. As you progress, the chapters will introduce you to more intricate dishes, allowing you to diversify your cooking skills and impress your friends and family.

A Journey Through Flavors

Explore the "Stir-Fry Sensations" and "Steamy Affairs" for a comprehensive look at two fundamental wok cooking techniques. These chapters are designed to expand your culinary repertoire, offering a range of recipes from classic stir-fries to steamed delicacies. Each recipe comes with detailed instructions, making it easy for beginners to follow and succeed.

Savor the Wok Experience

In "Savor the Flavor" and "Regional Wok Wonders," your culinary journey takes a deeper dive into the rich world of wok cooking. These chapters showcase the versatility of the wok, presenting recipes that range from soups and broths to regional specialties from across Asia. As you cook your way through these chapters, you'll gain a deeper appreciation for the diverse culinary traditions that the wok represents.

Planning and Preparing

Finally, "Meal Plans and Menus" offers practical advice for integrating wok cooking into your daily life. This chapter is particularly useful for planning meals, whether it's for a regular weeknight dinner or a special occasion. Use these plans as a starting point to mix and match recipes from earlier chapters, tailoring meals to your taste and the occasion.

Conclusion: Your Wok, Your Journey

Remember, "Wok Cookbook for Beginners" is more than a cookbook; it's a guide to a new way of cooking and experiencing food. Approach each recipe with an open mind and a willingness to experiment. The wok is a versatile tool, and with this book, you now have the knowledge to explore its full potential. So, open your cookbook, fire up your wok, and start your journey to becoming a wok master.

Chapter I: Wok Basics

The History of the Wok

The story of the wok begins in the mystical lands of China, where it originated over two thousand years ago. It's not just a cooking vessel; it's a symbol of Chinese culinary tradition, an artisan's tool that has stood the test of time. In its early days, the wok was a crucial utensil for common folk, who often had limited resources. Its unique shape - high, sloping sides, and a small base - made it versatile and efficient, perfect for a variety of cooking techniques with minimal fuel consumption.

The Wok's Journey Through Time and Cultures

As Chinese culture spread, so did the popularity of the wok. By the time of the Han Dynasty, it had become a staple in every household. The wok's journey through the centuries is a tale of adaptation and innovation. It wasn't just about stir-frying; it was used for boiling, steaming, deep-frying, and even smoking. Each dynasty added its own twist to wok cooking, enriching its history and versatility. As Chinese immigrants traveled, they took the wok with them, introducing it to new lands and cultures, making it a global icon in culinary history.

The Evolution of Wok Design

Initially, woks were made of cast iron, heavy and requiring meticulous care. However, as technology evolved, so did wok manufacturing. The introduction of carbon steel marked a significant evolution, offering a lighter, more manageable version without compromising on quality. Today, you'll find woks in various materials, each offering unique benefits, but the essence remains the same - a tool designed for efficiency and versatility.

The wok is more than just a tool for cooking; it's a cultural emblem that represents the philosophy of Chinese cooking. It's about harmony and balance - the yin and yang of flavors and textures. Wok cooking is a dance of heat, ingredients, and technique, all coming together in a single vessel. It's a testament to the ingenuity of early cooks who made the most of what they had, turning simple ingredients into culinary masterpieces.

Wok Cooking: A Reflection of Life

The wok's enduring popularity is a reflection of its ability to adapt to the needs of different eras and cultures. It's not just about the food; it's about the stories, the families, and the traditions that revolve around it. Every stir-fry, every steam, every deep-fry in a wok is a continuation of a centuries-old legacy, a legacy that you are now a part of.

As you embark on your journey with "Wok Cookbook for Beginners," remember that you're not just learning recipes; you're partaking in a rich, historical tradition. Every time you cook with a wok, you're honoring the legacy of countless cooks before you, from ancient China to modern kitchens around the world. The wok is not just a utensil; it's a bridge connecting past and present, a vessel carrying centuries of culinary wisdom into your home. Welcome to the world of wok cooking – a world where history sizzles in every dish.

Choosing Your Wok: A Buyer's Guide

Choosing Your Wok: A Buyer's Guide

Choosing the right wok is akin to finding a dance partner in the culinary ballet of wok cooking. It's about understanding its essence, its material, and how it complements your cooking style. The wok is not just a pan; it's a vessel that carries history, tradition, and flavor in each of its curves. When selecting a wok, you're not just buying a piece of cookware; you're investing in a tool that will transform your culinary experiences.

Materials and Their Magic

The journey to finding your perfect wok begins with understanding the materials. Traditional cast iron woks, known for their superior heat retention and even cooking, are the ancestors in the wok family. They are heavy, require seasoning, but offer a non-stick surface over time. Carbon steel woks are the most popular choice in modern kitchens. Lightweight, with excellent heat conduction, these woks respond quickly to temperature changes, making them ideal for the fast-paced stir-fry. Stainless steel woks, while not traditional, are gaining popularity for their durability and ease of maintenance, though they don't conduct heat as well as their counterparts.

The shape of the wok is as crucial as its material. The traditional round-bottomed wok is designed to sit in a wok ring on a gas stove, allowing the flame to heat the wok evenly. The flat-bottomed wok, on the other hand, is more versatile and compatible with electric and induction stovetops. It still offers good heat distribution, making it a practical choice for the modern kitchen.

Size Matters: Finding Your Fit

Size is another critical factor. A 12 to 14-inch wok is ideal for home kitchens, offering enough space to cook a meal for a family while being manageable and easy to handle. Larger woks may offer more cooking space but require more heat and can be cumbersome.

Handles: The Touch of Comfort

Handles are the touchpoint of your interaction with the wok. The traditional wok features two small, metal loop handles, requiring the use of potholders. Modern woks often come with one long wooden or plastic handle, like a skillet, making them easier to maneuver. Some woks feature a combination of one long handle and one loop handle, providing both ease of use and traditional handling.

Compatibility with Your Kitchen

Consider your stovetop when choosing a wok. If you have a gas stove, you can opt for either a round or flat-bottomed wok. For electric or induction stovetops, a flat-bottomed wok is more stable and efficient. If you're an outdoor cooking enthusiast, consider a wok that can be used on a grill or over an open flame for an authentic wok hei, the breath of the wok, experience.

The Lid: An Underrated Accessory

A lid is an often overlooked yet essential accessory for your wok. It's crucial for steaming and simmering dishes. Look for a dome-shaped lid that sits snugly inside the wok, allowing you to control the cooking environment perfectly.

Maintenance: The Key to Longevity

Finally, consider maintenance. Cast iron and carbon steel woks require seasoning and careful maintenance to develop and maintain their non-stick surfaces. Stainless steel woks, while easier to care for, don't offer the same natural non-stick qualities. Choose a wok that you're willing to care for, as a well-maintained wok becomes a trusted companion in your culinary adventures.

In your quest to master the art of wok cooking, choosing the right wok is a step towards success. It's not just about functionality; it's about finding a wok that resonates with your cooking style, your kitchen, and your culinary aspirations. When you find the right wok, it becomes more than a tool; it becomes a companion in your culinary journey, a bearer of flavors, and a keeper of traditions. Let your wok be a reflection of your culinary spirit, and together, create stir-fries, steamed delicacies, and sizzling sensations that delight, impress, and nourish.

The Essential Wok Toolkit

Equipping your kitchen for wok cooking is not just about having the right tools; it's about crafting an ensemble that works in harmony to bring out the best in your wok dishes. This essential toolkit is designed not only to complement your wok but also to enhance your overall cooking experience, ensuring that each stir-fry, steam, or simmer is a step towards culinary mastery.

Spatula and Ladle: The Conductor's Baton

The spatula and ladle are more than mere utensils; they are extensions of your hands. A wok spatula, with its wide, flat edge and long handle, is perfectly designed for the wok's curved sides, allowing for efficient stirring and flipping. The ladle is essential for soups, broths, and sauces, enabling precise control over liquids. Opt for materials that can withstand high heat and are comfortable to hold.

Steamer Rack and Bamboo Steamer: The Essence of Versatility

Steaming is an art form in wok cooking, and having the right tools is crucial. A metal steamer rack transforms your wok into a steamer, ideal for dishes like dumplings or vegetables. For a more traditional approach, a bamboo steamer offers layers of steaming space, infusing dishes with a subtle, woody aroma.

Wok Ring: The Foundation of Stability

For those using a round-bottomed wok on a conventional stove, a wok ring is a must. It provides stability, ensuring even heat distribution and safety while cooking. Choose a ring that fits your stove and wok size to avoid wobbling or uneven cooking.

Tongs and Chopsticks: Precision and Dexterity

Tongs and long cooking chopsticks are invaluable for handling ingredients with precision and dexterity. They are essential for tasks like turning pieces of meat or vegetables, removing food, or arranging ingredients in a steamer.

Knife and Cutting Board: The Prep Stars

A sharp chef's knife and a sturdy cutting board form the backbone of your wok toolkit. Efficient wok cooking requires ingredients to be cut uniformly for even cooking. Invest in quality to ensure ease and safety in your prep work.

Strainer and Oil Skimmer: The Unsung Heroes

A strainer or an oil skimmer is critical, especially for deep-frying or removing ingredients from broth. They help in draining excess oil or liquids, ensuring your dishes are not overly greasy or soggy.

A mortar and pestle allow you to grind fresh spices and herbs, releasing oils and flavors that pre-ground spices can't match. This simple tool can elevate your wok dishes with a depth of flavor that is unmistakably fresh.

Measuring Cups and Spoons: The Precision Tools

Consistency is key in cooking, and measuring cups and spoons bring precision to your recipes. They are particularly important for balancing flavors in marinades, sauces, and spice mixes.

Each tool in your wok toolkit requires care and attention. Maintain them as you would your wok, cleaning and storing them properly. Remember, a well-cared-for toolkit not only lasts longer but also improves your cooking experience.

Your wok toolkit is more than a collection of kitchen gadgets; it's the orchestra that plays the symphony of flavors in your wok. With these essential tools, you are equipped not just to cook but to create. They are your companions on your journey to wok mastery, each playing a vital role in bringing your culinary visions to life. So, gather your tools and let the wok magic begin!

Seasoning and Caring for Your Wok

Seasoning your wok is the inaugural step in your journey of wok mastery. It's a process that not only preps the surface for cooking but also begins the development of flavors unique to your culinary style. For those who choose carbon steel or cast iron, this step is critical. It involves coating the wok in a layer of oil and heating it to polymerize the surface. This is what creates that coveted non-stick patina that makes wok cooking a breeze. The wok's surface should be scrubbed clean, oiled, and heated until it starts to smoke. Then, it's cooled and repeated - this initial seasoning is a foundation upon which layers of flavor will build over time.

Ongoing Care: Beyond the Initial Season

Caring for your wok is like tending to a growing relationship; it requires consistent attention and evolves with experience. After each use, it should be cleaned with hot water and a soft sponge or brush—no soap, as it can strip the seasoning. If stubborn bits remain, warm water and a gentle scrub can help. Dry it immediately with heat to prevent rust. Then, coat it lightly with oil before storing. This ritual after each use helps maintain the non-stick surface and protects the metal.

Maintaining a wok is also about what not to do. The no-soap rule is crucial for preserving the patina, especially for non-coated woks. If rust spots do appear, don't despair. They can be scrubbed away with a little elbow grease; the wok can be re-seasoned as good as new. It's a forgiving process that reflects the wok's resilience and your growing understanding of its care.

Understanding the Patina's Evolution
With each use, the wok's patina darkens, enhancing its non-stick properties. This evolution is natural and expected—it's a sign of a well-used wok. Over time, it will develop a glossy black surface that rivals any non-stick pan and infuses your dishes with that ineffable wok hei, the essence of wok cooking.

A well-seasoned and cared-for wok is more than a cooking instrument; it's a culinary companion that evolves with you, reflecting your cooking journey in its sheen and surface. The flavors of meals past linger in its curves, ready to blend with today's ingredients to create something extraordinary. Treat it with respect and attentiveness, and it will serve you faithfully, meal after meal, year after year.

The Art of Stir-Frying: Techniques and Tips

The secret to impeccable stir-frying lies in mastering the heat. The high heat and quick cooking preserve the freshness of ingredients, seal in flavors, and create the coveted 'wok hei' — the breath of the wok. Begin by heating your wok until a drop of water vaporizes within seconds of contact. This is the stage where the wok whispers it's ready for the ingredients.

Harmony of Ingredients: Preparation Meets Execution

Before the wok meets the flame, preparation is key. Slice meats and vegetables uniformly to ensure even cooking. Marinate meats to enhance flavor and tenderness. Have all your ingredients within arm's reach, as the swift nature of stir-frying leaves no room for pause. Once you add oil — a high-smoke-point oil like peanut or grapeseed is preferred — swirl it around to coat the surface. This creates a non-stick layer, setting the stage for what's to come.

The Dance of Stir-Frying: A Symphony of Movements

The act of stir-frying is akin to a well-choreographed dance — it's swift, it's rhythmic, and it's done with confidence. Start by adding the ingredients that take the longest to cook, typically meats. They need space, so don't overcrowd the wok; cook in batches if necessary. Once they're seared and just shy of being fully cooked, set them aside.

Introduce hardy vegetables next, the ones that need more time to become tender. Keep them moving with assertive flicks of the wrist, allowing the heat to kiss every surface. As they reach their halfway point, introduce quicker-cooking vegetables, followed by aromatics like garlic, ginger, and green onions, which are prone to burning if added too early.

Layering Flavors: A Cascade of Additions

Now, it's time to reintroduce the meat back into the wok, mixing it with the vegetables. Pour in your sauces — soy, oyster, hoisin, or a custom mix — and watch as the high heat melds them into a rich coating for your stir-fry. If a thicker sauce is desired, a cornstarch slurry can be added at this stage. The sauce will bubble and thicken rapidly, so keep everything moving.

The Final Act: Perfecting the Toss

The final technique in stir-frying is the toss. It's not just about mixing; it's about aerating, allowing the heat to circulate through all the ingredients, giving them a light, smoky flavor that is the hallmark of great wok cooking. With the back-and-forth movement, the stir-fry comes to life, each ingredient infused with the flavors of the sauce and the smokiness of the wok.

The Artful Wok Warrior

In mastering the art of stir-frying, you become more than a cook — you're an artist, a warrior, wielding the wok with skill and precision. Remember, the best stir-fries are made not just with fresh ingredients and the right techniques, but with passion and presence. Each time you light the flame, you're not just cooking; you're creating a moment, a meal, a memory. So, arm yourself with these techniques, step up to the stove, and stir-fry with the heart of a wok warrior.

Flavor Boosters: Sauces, Marinades, and Spice Mixes

The Soul of Wok Cooking: Crafting Flavor Foundations

In the realm of wok cooking, the true magic lies in the flavors. Sauces, marinades, and spice mixes are the alchemists of the kitchen, transforming the simplest ingredients into a feast for the senses. They are the undercurrents of flavor that give wok dishes their soul, their depth, and their identity.

Sauces: The Liquid Artistry of the Wok

Sauces are the liquid artistry in the wok's canvas, providing moisture, sheen, and a complex layering of flavors. A masterful sauce balances the five taste elements: sweetness, sourness, saltiness, bitterness, and umami. Soy sauce offers saltiness and umami, while oyster sauce contributes a depth of flavor that's hard to replicate. For sweetness and tang, hoisin sauce and rice vinegar are irreplaceable, and a touch of sesame oil can add a nutty bitterness that rounds out a dish.

Creating a signature sauce involves understanding the interplay of these elements. Begin with a base—soy or oyster sauce—and build from there. Add sweetness with a spoonful of sugar or honey, sourness with vinegar or lime juice, and heat with chili paste or fresh peppers. The secret is in the simmer; let the sauce bubble in the wok to meld the flavors and thicken to a glaze that clings to your stir-fry, infusing every bite with your unique flavor signature.

Marinades: The Tender Whispers of Flavor

Marinades whisper flavors into the very fibers of your meats and vegetables, tenderizing them and infusing them with character. A good marinade is a symphony of acidic components like rice wine or lemon juice, savory elements like soy sauce or fish sauce, and aromatic enhancers like garlic, ginger, and scallions.

To marinate is to be patient; it's to allow time for the ingredients to absorb and become one with the flavors. Even a brief 30-minute marinade can transform the taste and texture of your ingredients, making them ready to take center stage in your wok.

Spice Mixes: The Sprinkling of Wok Alchemy

Spice mixes are the final flourish, the sprinkling of alchemy that completes the wok dish. They're a mosaic of ground spices and dried herbs that, when heated, release oils and aromatics into your cooking. A simple mix might begin with the heat of Szechuan peppercorns, the warmth of cinnamon, and the earthiness of star anise. To this, you can add the brightness of coriander, the bite of fennel seeds, and the mysterious depth of cloves.

Each spice mix you create becomes a signature, a secret blend that is uniquely yours, elevating your dishes from the everyday to the extraordinary. Use these mixes sparingly at first, allowing the natural taste of your ingredients to shine, and adjust as your palate guides you.

Conclusion: The Quintessence of Flavor

The creation of sauces, marinades, and spice mixes is not just cooking; it's an art form that requires practice, intuition, and a willingness to experiment. It's a journey of discovery that leads to the heart of wok cooking—the unending quest for the perfect balance of flavors. So, wield these flavor boosters like an artist wields a brush, and paint your wok dishes with the quintessence of taste.

Chapter II: Quick Start Guide

15-Minute Wok Recipes for Busy Weeknights

Ginger-Soy Shrimp Stir-Fry

- **Preparation time:** 15 minutes
- **Ingredients:** 1 lb shrimp, peeled and deveined; 2 tbsp soy sauce; 1 tbsp freshly grated ginger; 2 garlic cloves, minced; 1 cup mixed bell peppers, thinly sliced; 1/2 cup green onions, chopped.
- **Servings:** 4
- **Cooking method:** Wok Stir-Fry
- **Procedure:** 1. Marinate shrimp in soy sauce, ginger, and garlic; 2. Heat oil in wok, add shrimp, stir-fry for 3-4 minutes; 3. Add bell peppers, cook for 2 minutes in wok; 4. Stir in green onions before serving.
- **Nutritional values:** Estimated Calories: 200, Protein: 24g, Carbohydrates: 6g, Fat: 8g, Fiber: 2g.

Sweet and Spicy Chicken

- **Preparation time:** 15 minutes
- **Ingredients:** 1 lb chicken breast, thinly sliced; 2 tbsp honey; 1 tbsp sriracha; 1 tbsp rice wine vinegar; 1 cup snow peas; 1/4 cup roasted peanuts.
- **Servings:** 4
- **Cooking method:** Wok Stir-Fry
- **Procedure:** 1. Combine chicken with honey and sriracha; 2. Cook chicken in hot wok until golden; 3. Add snow peas and vinegar; 4. Garnish with peanuts in wok.
- **Nutritional values:** Estimated Calories: 250, Protein: 26g, Carbohydrates: 15g, Fat: 10g, Fiber: 2g.

Beef and Broccoli in Oyster Sauce

- **Preparation time:** 15 minutes
- **Ingredients:** 1 lb sliced beef, 2 cups broccoli florets, 3 tbsp oyster sauce, 2 garlic cloves, minced, 1 tbsp ginger, minced.
- **Servings:** 4
- **Cooking method:** Wok Stir-Fry
- **Procedure:** 1. Sauté beef, garlic, and ginger in wok; 2. Add broccoli and oyster sauce; 3. Stir-fry in wok until beef is cooked and broccoli is tender.

- **Nutritional values:** Estimated Calories: 300, Protein: 25g, Carbohydrates: 20g, Fat: 15g, Fiber: 4g.

Szechuan Tofu and Green Bean

- **Preparation time:** 15 minutes
- **Ingredients:** 1 block firm tofu, diced, 1 cup green beans, trimmed, 2 tbsp Szechuan sauce, 1 tsp Szechuan peppercorns, crushed, 2 garlic cloves, minced.
- **Servings:** 4
- **Cooking method:** Wok Stir-Fry
- **Procedure:** 1. Fry tofu and green beans in wok with oil; 2. Add garlic and peppercorns; 3. Toss in Szechuan sauce; 4. Cook in wok until beans are tender.
- **Nutritional values:** Estimated Calories: 200, Protein: 12g, Carbohydrates: 10g, Fat: 12g, Fiber: 3g.

Garlic Mushroom and Bok Choy Sauté

- **Preparation time:** 15 minutes
- **Ingredients:** 2 cups mixed mushrooms, sliced, 2 bok choy heads, chopped, 3 garlic cloves, minced, 2 tbsp soy sauce, 1 tsp sesame oil.
- **Servings:** 4
- **Cooking method:** Wok Sauté
- **Procedure:** 1. Cook mushrooms and garlic in wok; 2. Add bok choy and soy sauce; 3. Drizzle with sesame oil before serving.
- **Nutritional values:** Estimated Calories: 150, Protein: 6g, Carbohydrates: 15g, Fat: 8g, Fiber: 4g.

Thai Basil Pork

- **Preparation time:** 15 minutes
- **Ingredients:** 1 lb ground pork, 1 cup Thai basil leaves, 2 tbsp fish sauce, 1 tbsp brown sugar, 1 red chili, sliced.
- **Servings:** 4
- **Cooking method:** Wok Stir-Fry
- **Procedure:** 1. Cook pork and chili in wok; 2. Add fish sauce and sugar; 3. Stir in basil and cook until wilted in wok.
- **Nutritional values:** Estimated Calories: 280, Protein: 22g, Carbohydrates: 10g, Fat: 18g, Fiber: 1g.

Orange-Glazed Salmon Stir-Fry

- **Preparation time:** 15 minutes
- **Ingredients:** 1 lb salmon, cubed, 1/2 cup orange juice, 2 tbsp soy sauce, 2 garlic cloves, minced, 2 cups stir-fry vegetables.
- **Servings:** 4
- **Cooking method:** Wok Stir-Fry
- **Procedure:** 1. Glaze salmon with orange juice and soy sauce; 2. Stir-fry salmon in wok; 3. Add vegetables and cook until tender.
- **Nutritional values:** Estimated Calories: 300, Protein: 23g, Carbohydrates: 15g, Fat: 16g, Fiber: 3g.

Stir-Fried Rice Noodles with Vegetables

- **Preparation time:** 15 minutes
- **Ingredients:** 2 cups rice noodles, soaked, 2 tbsp soy sauce, 1 tbsp lime juice, 2 garlic cloves, minced, 1 cup bean sprouts, 1/4 cup scallions, sliced.
- **Servings:** 4
- **Cooking method:** Wok Stir-Fry
- **Procedure:** 1. Cook noodles and vegetables in wok; 2. Add soy sauce and garlic; 3. Finish with lime juice.

- **Nutritional values:** Estimated Calories: 220, Protein: 4g, Carbohydrates: 42g, Fat: 4g, Fiber: 2g.

Wok Recipes with 5 Ingredients or Less

Classic Garlic Broccoli Stir-Fry

- **Preparation time:** 10 minutes
- **Ingredients:** 2 cups broccoli florets, 3 minced garlic cloves, 2 tbsp soy sauce, 1 tbsp olive oil, 1 tsp sesame seeds.
- **Servings:** 2
- **Mode of cooking:** Wok Stir-Fry
- **Procedure:** 1. Heat oil in wok; 2. Add garlic, cook until fragrant; 3. Stir-fry broccoli; 4. Add soy sauce; 5. Garnish with sesame seeds.
- **Nutritional values:** Calories: 90, Protein: 3g, Carbohydrates: 10g, Fat: 5g, Fiber: 3g.

Spicy Szechuan Green Beans

- **Preparation time:** 12 minutes
- **Ingredients:** 2 cups green beans, 2 tbsp Szechuan sauce, 1 tbsp vegetable oil, 1 tsp chili flakes, 1 tsp minced ginger.
- **Servings:** 2
- **Mode of cooking:** Wok Stir-Fry
- **Procedure:** 1. Heat oil in wok; 2. Add ginger and chili; 3. Add green beans; 4. Toss with Szechuan sauce.
- **Nutritional values:** Calories: 100, Protein: 2g, Carbohydrates: 12g, Fat: 6g, Fiber: 4g.

Simple Pepper Beef

- **Preparation time:** 15 minutes
- **Ingredients:** 1 lb beef strips, 2 sliced bell peppers, 2 tbsp oyster sauce, 1 tbsp vegetable oil, 1 tsp black pepper.
- **Servings:** 4
- **Mode of cooking:** Wok Stir-Fry
- **Procedure:** 1. Cook beef in wok; 2. Add bell peppers; 3. Season with oyster sauce and pepper.
- **Nutritional values:** Calories: 220, Protein: 25g, Carbohydrates: 9g, Fat: 10g, Fiber: 2g.

Honey Glazed Ginger Shrimp

- **Preparation time:** 15 minutes
- **Ingredients:** 1 lb shrimp, 2 tbsp honey, 1 tbsp soy sauce, 1 tsp minced ginger, 1 tbsp olive oil.
- **Servings:** 4
- **Mode of cooking:** Wok Stir-Fry
- **Procedure:** 1. Mix honey, soy sauce, and ginger; 2. Cook shrimp in wok; 3. Glaze with honey mixture.
- **Nutritional values:** Calories: 180, Protein: 24g, Carbohydrates: 10g, Fat: 6g, Fiber: 0g.
-

Sweet and Sour Pineapple Pork

- **Preparation time:** 15 minutes
- **Ingredients:** 1 lb pork tenderloin, 1 cup pineapple chunks, 2 tbsp sweet and sour sauce, 1 tbsp vegetable oil, 1 sliced red bell pepper.
- **Servings:** 4
- **Mode of cooking:** Wok Stir-Fry
- **Procedure:** 1. Cook pork in wok; 2. Add bell pepper and pineapple; 3. Toss with sauce.
- **Nutritional values:** Calories: 250, Protein: 25g, Carbohydrates: 18g, Fat: 8g, Fiber: 1g.

Stir-Fried Tofu with Soy and Garlic

- **Preparation time:** 10 minutes
- **Ingredients:** 1 block firm tofu, 2 tbsp soy sauce, 3 minced garlic cloves, 1 tbsp sesame oil, 1 chopped green onion.
- **Servings:** 2
- **Mode of cooking:** Wok Stir-Fry
- **Procedure:** 1. Cook garlic in wok; 2. Add tofu; 3. Stir in soy sauce; 4. Garnish with green onion.
- **Nutritional values:** Calories: 200, Protein: 12g, Carbohydrates: 7g, Fat: 14g, Fiber: 1g.

Chili Garlic Eggplant

- **Preparation time:** 15 minutes
- **Ingredients:** 2 medium eggplants, 2 tbsp chili garlic sauce, 1 tbsp soy sauce, 1 tbsp vegetable oil, 1 tsp sesame seeds.
- **Servings:** 2
- **Mode of cooking:** Wok Stir-Fry
- **Procedure:** 1. Cook eggplant in wok; 2. Stir in sauces; 3. Sprinkle with sesame seeds.
- **Nutritional values:** Calories: 120, Protein: 3g, Carbohydrates: 20g, Fat: 5g, Fiber: 6g.

Teriyaki Salmon and Broccoli

- **Preparation time:** 15 minutes
- **Ingredients:** 2 salmon fillets, 2 cups broccoli florets, 3 tbsp teriyaki sauce, 1 tbsp olive oil, 1 tsp sesame seeds.
- **Servings:** 2
- **Mode of cooking:** Wok Stir-Fry
- **Procedure:** 1. Sear salmon in wok; 2. Add broccoli; 3. Glaze with teriyaki; 4. Garnish with sesame seeds.
- **Nutritional values:** Calories: 300, Protein: 23g, Carbohydrates: 12g, Fat: 17g, Fiber: 3g.

Nutritional Information and Healthy Swaps

Basil Zucchini and Chicken Stir-Fry

- **Preparation time:** 15 minutes
- **Ingredients:** 1 lb chicken breast (sliced), 2 large zucchinis (spiraled), 1 cup fresh basil leaves, 2 tbsp low-sodium soy sauce, 1 tbsp olive oil.
- **Servings:** 4
- **Cooking method:** Wok Stir-Fry
- **Procedure:** 1. Sauté chicken in wok with olive oil; 2. Add zucchini noodles to the wok; 3. Season with soy sauce; 4. Incorporate basil leaves at the end.
- **Nutritional values:** Calories: 190, Protein: 26g, Carbohydrates: 5g, Fat: 7g, Fiber: 2g.

Turmeric Cauliflower Fried Rice

Preparation time: 15 minutes
- **Ingredients:** 2 cups cauliflower rice, 1/2 cup peas, 1/2 cup diced carrots, 1 tsp turmeric, 1 tbsp coconut oil.
- **Servings:** 2
- **Cooking method:** Wok Stir-Fry
- **Procedure:** 1. Heat coconut oil in wok; 2. Add turmeric, peas, and carrots to the wok; 3. Stir in cauliflower rice; 4. Cook in the wok until tender.
- **Nutritional values:** Calories: 120, Protein: 4g, Carbohydrates: 10g, Fat: 7g, Fiber: 3g.

Lemon Garlic Shrimp and Broccolini

- **Preparation time:** 12 minutes
- **Ingredients:** 1 lb shrimp (peeled), 2 cups broccolini, 2 garlic cloves (minced), Juice of 1 lemon, 1 tbsp avocado oil.
- **Servings:** 4
- **Cooking method:** Wok Stir-Fry
- **Procedure:** 1. Cook garlic in wok with avocado oil; 2. Add shrimp and broccolini to the wok; 3. Drizzle with lemon juice while cooking.
- **Nutritional values:** Calories: 180, Protein: 24g, Carbohydrates: 6g, Fat: 8g, Fiber: 2g.

Ginger Soy Mushroom Stir-Fry

- **Preparation time:** 12 minutes
- **Ingredients:** 2 cups mixed mushrooms, 1 tbsp low-sodium soy sauce, 1 tsp minced ginger, 1 tbsp grapeseed oil, 1 green onion (sliced).
- **Servings:** 2
- **Cooking method:** Wok Stir-Fry
- **Procedure:** 1. Sauté ginger in wok with grapeseed oil; 2. Add mushrooms to the wok; 3. Season with soy sauce; 4. Garnish with green onion after stir-frying.
- **Nutritional values:** Calories: 100, Protein: 3g, Carbohydrates: 8g, Fat: 7g, Fiber: 2g.

Spicy Tofu and Green Bean Stir-Fry

- **Preparation time:** 15 minutes
- **Ingredients:** 1 block firm tofu (cubed), 2 cups green beans, 1 tbsp chili paste, 1 tsp sesame oil, 1 tsp crushed garlic.
- **Servings:** 4
- **Cooking method:** Wok Stir-Fry
- **Procedure:** 1. Brown tofu in wok with sesame oil; 2. Add green beans and garlic to the wok; 3. Stir in chili paste while stir-frying.
- **Nutritional values:** Calories: 150, Protein: 10g, Carbohydrates: 10g, Fat: 9g, Fiber: 3g.

Hoisin Glazed Salmon with Snap Peas

- **Preparation time:** 15 minutes
- **Ingredients:** 2 salmon fillets, 1 cup snap peas, 2 tbsp hoisin sauce, 1 tsp olive oil, 1 tsp sesame seeds.
- **Servings:** 2
- **Cooking method:** Wok Stir-Fry
- **Procedure:** 1. Sear salmon in wok with olive oil; 2. Add snap peas to the wok; 3. Glaze with hoisin sauce; 4. Sprinkle sesame seeds after cooking.
- **Nutritional values:** Calories: 300, Protein: 23g, Carbohydrates: 15g, Fat: 16g, Fiber: 2g.

Bok Choy and Shiitake Mushroom Stir-Fry

- **Preparation time:** 12 minutes
- **Ingredients:** 3 cups baby bok choy, 1 cup shiitake mushrooms, 1 tbsp tamari, 1 tsp garlic (minced), 1 tbsp canola oil.
- **Servings:** 2
- **Cooking method:** Wok Stir-Fry
- **Procedure:** 1. Heat canola oil in wok; 2. Add garlic and mushrooms to the wok; 3. Stir in bok choy; 4. Season with tamari while cooking.
- **Nutritional values:** Calories: 90, Protein: 4g, Carbohydrates: 8g, Fat: 5g, Fiber: 3g.

Orange Ginger Beef Stir-Fry

- **Preparation time:** 15 minutes
- **Ingredients:** 1 lb lean beef strips, Juice of 1 orange, 1 tbsp minced ginger, 1 red bell pepper (sliced), 1 tsp canola oil.
- **Servings:** 4
- **Cooking method:** Wok Stir-Fry
- **Procedure:** 1. Stir-fry beef and ginger in wok with canola oil; 2. Add bell pepper to the wok; 3. Drizzle with orange juice while cooking.
- **Nutritional values:** Calories: 220, Protein: 25g, Carbohydrates: 10g, Fat: 9g, Fiber: 1g.

Chapter III: Stir-Fry Sensations

Chicken Stir-Fries

Citrus Ginger Chicken Stir-Fry

- **Preparation time:** 15 minutes
- **Ingredients:** 1 lb chicken breast (thinly sliced), 1 orange (juice and zest), 1 tbsp minced ginger, 1 red bell pepper (sliced), 1 tbsp olive oil.
  - **Servings:** 4
- **Cooking method:** Wok Stir-Fry
- **Procedure:** 1. Sauté ginger in wok with olive oil; 2. Add chicken, cook until halfway done; 3. Introduce bell pepper and orange zest; 4. Pour in orange juice, stir until chicken is fully cooked.
- **Nutritional values:** Calories: 200, Protein: 26g, Carbohydrates: 8g, Fat: 8g, Fiber: 2g.

Honey Sriracha Chicken

- **Preparation time:** 15 minutes
- **Ingredients:** 1 lb chicken thighs (cubed), 2 tbsp honey, 1 tbsp sriracha, 1 cup snap peas, 1 tbsp canola oil.
  - **Servings:** 4
- **Cooking method:** Wok Stir-Fry
- **Procedure:** 1. Heat canola oil in wok; 2. Brown chicken cubes; 3. Mix in honey and sriracha; 4. Add snap peas, stir until glazed and tender.
- **Nutritional values:** Calories: 250, Protein: 24g, Carbohydrates: 15g, Fat: 10g, Fiber: 1g.

Basil and Tomato Chicken

- **Preparation time:** 15 minutes
- **Ingredients:** 1 lb chicken tenders, 1 cup cherry tomatoes (halved), 1/2 cup fresh basil (torn), 1 tbsp balsamic vinegar, 1 tsp olive oil.
  - **Servings:** 4
- **Cooking method:** Wok Stir-Fry
- **Procedure:** 1. Cook chicken in wok with olive oil until golden; 2. Add tomatoes and balsamic vinegar; 3. Stir in basil before serving.
- **Nutritional values:** Calories: 190, Protein: 28g, Carbohydrates: 6g, Fat: 6g, Fiber: 1g.

Lemongrass Chicken Stir-Fry

- **Preparation time:** 15 minutes
- **Ingredients:** 1 lb chicken breast (sliced), 1 stalk lemongrass (minced), 1 cup broccoli florets, 2 tbsp soy sauce, 1 tbsp sesame oil.
  - **Servings:** 4
- **Cooking method:** Wok Stir-Fry
- **Procedure:** 1. Sauté lemongrass in wok with sesame oil; 2. Add chicken, stir until almost cooked; 3. Introduce broccoli, cook with soy sauce until tender.
- **Nutritional values:** Calories: 210, Protein: 27g, Carbohydrates: 7g, Fat: 9g, Fiber: 2g.

Spicy Peanut Chicken

- **Preparation time:** 15 minutes
- **Ingredients:** 1 lb diced chicken breast, 1/4 cup peanut butter, 1 tbsp chili garlic sauce, 1 red bell pepper (diced), 1 tbsp vegetable oil.
  - **Servings:** 4
- **Cooking method:** Wok Stir-Fry
- **Procedure:** 1. Heat oil, cook chicken in wok; 2. Blend peanut butter and chili sauce; 3. Toss bell pepper and peanut mixture with chicken.
- **Nutritional values:** Calories: 280, Protein: 29g, Carbohydrates: 8g, Fat: 15g, Fiber: 2g.

Garlic Lime Chicken with Asparagus

- **Preparation time:** 15 minutes
- **Ingredients:** 1 lb chicken thighs (cut into strips), 1 bunch asparagus (trimmed), 2 garlic cloves (minced), Juice of 1 lime, 1 tbsp grapeseed oil.
  - **Servings:** 4
- **Cooking method:** Wok Stir-Fry
- **Procedure:** 1. Cook garlic and chicken in wok with grapeseed oil; 2. Add asparagus, stir until vibrant; 3. Splash lime juice over the mix.
- **Nutritional values:** Calories: 230, Protein: 22g, Carbohydrates: 4g, Fat: 14g, Fiber: 2g.

Soy Glazed Chicken with Mushrooms

- **Preparation time:** 15 minutes
- **Ingredients:** 1 lb chicken breast (thinly sliced), 2 cups sliced mushrooms, 2 tbsp low-sodium soy sauce, 1 tsp ginger (minced), 1 tbsp olive oil.
- **Servings:** 4
- **Cooking method:** Wok Stir-Fry
- **Procedure:** 1. Sauté ginger in wok with olive oil; 2. Add chicken, cook until half done; 3. Stir in mushrooms and soy sauce; 4. Cook until chicken is fully done.
- **Nutritional values:** Calories: 210, Protein: 27g, Carbohydrates: 5g, Fat: 9g, Fiber: 1g.

Sweet Chili Chicken and Green Beans

- **Preparation time:** 15 minutes
- **Ingredients:** 1 lb chicken tenders, 1 cup green beans (trimmed), 3 tbsp sweet chili sauce, 1 tsp sesame oil, 1 tsp garlic (minced).
- **Servings:** 4
- **Cooking method:** Wok Stir-Fry
- **Procedure:** 1. Heat sesame oil and garlic in wok; 2. Add chicken, cook until almost done; 3. Introduce green beans and sweet chili sauce; 4. Stir-fry until chicken is cooked and beans are crisp-tender.
- **Nutritional values:** Calories: 220, Protein: 25g, Carbohydrates: 15g, Fat: 7g, Fiber: 1g.

Beef Stir-Fries

Black Bean Beef with Peppers

- **Preparation time:** 15 minutes
- **Ingredients:** 1 lb beef sirloin (thinly sliced), 1 red bell pepper (sliced), 1 green bell pepper (sliced), 2 tbsp black bean sauce, 1 tsp sesame oil.
- **Servings:** 4
- **Cooking method:** Wok Stir-Fry
-
-
- **Procedure:** 1. Heat sesame oil in wok; 2. Stir-fry beef until brown; 3. Add bell peppers; 4. Coat with black bean sauce; 5. Stir until peppers are tender.
- **Nutritional values:** Calories: 250, Protein: 25g, Carbohydrates: 8g, Fat: 14g, Fiber: 2g.

Mongolian Beef with Scallions

- **Preparation time:** 15 minutes
- **Ingredients:** 1 lb flank steak (sliced), 3 green onions (chopped), 2 tbsp soy sauce, 1 tbsp brown sugar, 1 tsp grated ginger.
- **Servings:** 4
- **Cooking method:** Wok Stir-Fry
- **Procedure:** 1. Mix soy sauce, sugar, and ginger; 2. Sauté beef in wok; 3. Pour sauce over beef; 4. Add green onions; 5. Cook until onions are slightly soft.
- **Nutritional values:** Calories: 270, Protein: 28g, Carbohydrates: 10g, Fat: 13g, Fiber: 1g.

Szechuan Beef with Snow Peas

- **Preparation time:** 15 minutes
- **Ingredients:** 1 lb beef tenderloin (sliced), 1 cup snow peas, 2 tbsp Szechuan sauce, 1 tsp peanut oil, 1 tsp minced garlic.
- **Servings:** 4
- **Cooking method:** Wok Stir-Fry
- **Procedure:** 1. Heat oil and garlic in wok; 2. Add beef, cook until seared; 3. Introduce snow peas; 4. Toss with Szechuan sauce; 5. Stir until peas are crisp.

- **Nutritional values:** Calories: 280, Protein: 26g, Carbohydrates: 9g, Fat: 16g, Fiber: 2g.

Beef and Broccoli in Oyster Sauce

- **Preparation time:** 15 minutes
- **Ingredients:** 1 lb beef round (sliced), 2 cups broccoli florets, 3 tbsp oyster sauce, 1 tbsp vegetable oil, 1 tsp soy sauce.
- **Servings:** 4
- **Cooking method:** Wok Stir-Fry
- **Procedure:** 1. Sauté beef in wok with oil; 2. Add broccoli, stir-fry until bright green; 3. Blend in oyster and soy sauces; 4. Cook until beef is glazed.
- **Nutritional values:** Calories: 240, Protein: 27g, Carbohydrates: 8g, Fat: 12g, Fiber: 3g.

Ginger Beef Stir-Fry with Red Onion

- **Preparation time:** 15 minutes
- **Ingredients:** 1 lb skirt steak (sliced), 1 red onion (sliced), 2 tbsp grated ginger, 1 tbsp hoisin sauce, 1 tsp sesame seeds.
- **Servings:** 4
- **Cooking method:** Wok Stir-Fry
- **Procedure:** 1. Stir-fry ginger and onion in wok; 2. Add beef, cook until nearly done; 3. Glaze with hoisin sauce; 4. Sprinkle sesame seeds before serving.
- **Nutritional values:** Calories: 260, Protein: 24g, Carbohydrates: 12g, Fat: 14g, Fiber: 1g.

Thai Basil and Chili Beef

- **Preparation time:** 15 minutes
- **Ingredients:** 1 lb ground beef, 1 cup Thai basil leaves, 1 red chili (sliced), 2 tbsp fish sauce, 1 tsp coconut oil.
- **Servings:** 4
- **Cooking method:** Wok Stir-Fry
- **Procedure:** 1. Cook beef with chili in wok; 2. Add fish sauce for flavor; 3. Stir in basil leaves; 4. Cook until basil wilts and beef is cooked through.
- **Nutritional values:** Calories: 300, Protein: 20g, Carbohydrates: 4g, Fat: 22g, Fiber: 1g.

Honey Soy Beef with Carrots

- **Preparation time:** 15 minutes
- **Ingredients:** 1 lb lean beef strips, 2 carrots (julienned), 2 tbsp soy sauce, 1 tbsp honey, 1 tsp olive oil.
- **Servings:** 4
- **Cooking method:** Wok Stir-Fry
- **Procedure:** 1. Heat oil in wok, stir-fry carrots; 2. Add beef, cook until brown; 3. Mix in honey and soy sauce; 4. Cook until sauce thickens slightly.
- **Nutritional values:** Calories: 220, Protein: 25g, Carbohydrates: 10g, Fat: 9g, Fiber: 2g.

Pepper Steak with Onions

- **Preparation time:** 15 minutes
- **Ingredients:** 1 lb sirloin steak (sliced), 2 bell peppers (sliced), 1 onion (sliced), 2 tbsp Worcestershire sauce, 1 tbsp olive oil.
- **Servings:** 4
- **Cooking method:** Wok Stir-Fry
- **Procedure:** 1. Sauté onion and peppers in wok with olive oil; 2. Introduce steak, cook until seared; 3. Drizzle with Worcestershire sauce; 4. Stir until well combined.
- **Nutritional values:** Calories: 250, Protein: 26g, Carbohydrates: 8g, Fat: 13g, Fiber: 2g.

Pork Stir-Fries

Honey Garlic Pork Stir-Fry

- **Preparation time:** 15 minutes
- **Ingredients:** 1 lb pork tenderloin (sliced), 2 tbsp honey, 2 garlic cloves (minced), 1 red bell pepper (sliced), 1 tbsp soy sauce.
- **Servings:** 4
- **Cooking method:** Wok Stir-Fry
- **Procedure:** 1. Stir-fry garlic and pork in wok; 2. Mix in bell pepper; 3. Drizzle with honey and soy sauce; 4. Cook until pork is glazed and tender.
- **Nutritional values:** Calories: 240, Protein: 25g, Carbohydrates: 15g, Fat: 9g, Fiber: 1g.

Spicy Szechuan Pork with Green Beans

- **Preparation time:** 15 minutes
- **Ingredients:** 1 lb ground pork, 2 cups green beans, 1 tbsp Szechuan sauce, 1 tsp vegetable oil, 1 tsp ginger (minced).
- **Servings:** 4
- **Cooking method:** Wok Stir-Fry
- **Procedure:** 1. Brown pork with ginger in wok; 2. Add green beans; 3. Toss with Szechuan sauce; 4. Stir-fry until beans are crisp-tender.
- **Nutritional values:** Calories: 280, Protein: 22g, Carbohydrates: 8g, Fat: 18g, Fiber: 3g.

Pork and Pineapple Stir-Fry

- **Preparation time:** 15 minutes
- **Ingredients:** 1 lb pork strips, 1 cup pineapple chunks, 1 bell pepper (sliced), 2 tbsp teriyaki sauce, 1 tsp sesame oil.
- **Servings:** 4
- **Cooking method:** Wok Stir-Fry
- **Procedure:** 1. Sauté pork in wok with sesame oil; 2. Introduce pineapple and bell pepper; 3. Glaze with teriyaki sauce.
- **Nutritional values:** Calories: 230, Protein: 24g, Carbohydrates: 15g, Fat: 8g, Fiber: 2g.

Black Pepper Pork Stir-Fry

- **Preparation time:** 15 minutes
- **Ingredients:** 1 lb pork loin (sliced), 1 tbsp black pepper, 1 onion (sliced), 2 tbsp oyster sauce, 1 tsp olive oil.
- **Servings:** 4
- **Cooking method:** Wok Stir-Fry
- **Procedure:** 1. Cook onion and pork in wok with olive oil; 2. Season with black pepper; 3. Finish with oyster sauce.
- **Nutritional values:** Calories: 220, Protein: 26g, Carbohydrates: 9g, Fat: 10g, Fiber: 1g.

Lemongrass Pork with Snap Peas

- **Preparation time:** 15 minutes
- **Ingredients:** 1 lb pork shoulder (sliced), 1 stalk lemongrass (minced), 1 cup snap peas, 2 tbsp fish sauce, 1 tsp canola oil.
- **Servings:** 4
- **Cooking method:** Wok Stir-Fry
- **Procedure:** 1. Stir-fry lemongrass and pork in wok; 2. Add snap peas; 3. Season with fish sauce; 4. Cook until peas are vibrant.
- **Nutritional values:** Calories: 250, Protein: 23g, Carbohydrates: 6g, Fat: 15g, Fiber: 2g.

Sweet and Sour Pork

- **Preparation time:** 15 minutes
- **Ingredients:** 1 lb pork belly (cubed), 1/2 cup sweet and sour sauce, 1 green bell pepper (diced), 1 red onion (diced), 1 tbsp vegetable oil.
- **Servings:** 4
- **Cooking method:** Wok Stir-Fry
- **Procedure:** 1. Brown pork in wok with oil; 2. Add bell pepper and onion; 3. Coat with sweet and sour sauce; 4. Stir-fry until veggies are soft.
- **Nutritional values:** Calories: 310, Protein: 14g, Carbohydrates: 20g, Fat: 20g, Fiber: 1g.

Thai Basil Pork

- **Preparation time:** 15 minutes
- **Ingredients:** 1 lb ground pork, 1 cup Thai basil leaves, 2 tbsp soy sauce, 1 red chili (sliced), 1 tbsp fish sauce.
- **Servings:** 4
- **Cooking method:** Wok Stir-Fry
- **Procedure:** 1. Cook pork with chili in wok; 2. Add Thai basil; 3. Season with soy and fish sauces; 4. Stir until basil is wilted.
- **Nutritional values:** Calories: 270, Protein: 22g, Carbohydrates: 3g, Fat: 19g, Fiber: 1g.

Hoisin Pork with Broccoli

- **Preparation time:** 15 minutes
- **Ingredients:** 1 lb pork fillet (sliced), 2 cups broccoli florets, 3 tbsp hoisin sauce, 1 tsp garlic (minced), 1 tbsp grapeseed oil.
- **Servings:** 4
- **Cooking method:** Wok Stir-Fry
- **Procedure:** 1. Sauté garlic and pork in wok with oil; 2. Add broccoli; 3. Glaze with hoisin sauce; 4. Cook until pork is tender and broccoli is crisp.
- **Nutritional values:** Calories: 240, Protein: 26g, Carbohydrates: 10g, Fat: 12g, Fiber: 3g.

Seafood Stir-Fries

Spicy Shrimp and Bell Pepper Stir-Fry

- **Preparation time:** 15 minutes
- **Ingredients:** 1 lb shrimp (peeled and deveined), 2 bell peppers (sliced), 1 tbsp sriracha sauce, 1 tsp garlic (minced), 1 tbsp soy sauce.
- **Servings:** 4
- **Cooking method:** Wok Stir-Fry
- **Procedure:** 1. Stir-fry garlic in wok; 2. Add shrimp, cook until pink; 3. Introduce bell peppers; 4. Season with sriracha and soy sauce; 5. Stir until veggies are tender.

- **Nutritional values:** Calories: 180, Protein: 24g, Carbohydrates: 6g, Fat: 7g, Fiber: 2g.

Garlic Lemon Scallops with Asparagus

- **Preparation time:** 15 minutes
- **Ingredients:** 1 lb scallops, 2 cups asparagus (chopped), 2 garlic cloves (minced), Juice of 1 lemon, 1 tbsp olive oil.
- **Servings:** 4
- **Cooking method:** Wok Stir-Fry
- **Procedure:** 1. Heat olive oil, sauté garlic in wok; 2. Add scallops, cook until golden; 3. Stir in asparagus; 4. Drizzle with lemon juice; 5. Cook until asparagus is crisp-tender.
- **Nutritional values:** Calories: 200, Protein: 23g, Carbohydrates: 5g, Fat: 10g, Fiber: 2g.

Ginger Soy Salmon Stir-Fry

- **Preparation time:** 15 minutes
- **Ingredients:** 1 lb salmon (cubed), 2 tbsp soy sauce, 1 tsp grated ginger, 1 cup snap peas, 1 tsp sesame oil.
- **Servings:** 4
- **Cooking method:** Wok Stir-Fry
- **Procedure:** 1. Marinate salmon in soy sauce and ginger; 2. Heat sesame oil in wok; 3. Add salmon, cook briefly; 4. Introduce snap peas; 5. Stir-fry until salmon is cooked through.
- **Nutritional values:** Calories: 240, Protein: 23g, Carbohydrates: 7g, Fat: 13g, Fiber: 2g.

Chili Lime Tilapia with Zucchini

- **Preparation time:** 15 minutes
- **Ingredients:** 1 lb tilapia fillets (sliced), 2 zucchinis (sliced), 1 tbsp chili powder, Juice of 1 lime, 1 tbsp canola oil.
- **Servings:** 4
- **Cooking method:** Wok Stir-Fry
- **Procedure:** 1. Season tilapia with chili powder; 2. Heat oil in wok; 3. Add tilapia, cook until opaque; 4. Stir in zucchini; 5. Squeeze lime juice over the stir-fry.
- **Nutritional values:** Calories: 180, Protein: 21g, Carbohydrates: 6g, Fat: 8g, Fiber: 2g.

Sesame Garlic Cod Stir-Fry

- **Preparation time:** 15 minutes
- **Ingredients:** 1 lb cod (cut into pieces), 1 tbsp sesame oil, 2 garlic cloves (minced), 1 red bell pepper (sliced), 2 tbsp soy sauce.
- **Servings:** 4
- **Cooking method:** Wok Stir-Fry
- **Procedure:** 1. Cook garlic in sesame oil in wok; 2. Add cod, stir until slightly cooked; 3. Introduce bell pepper; 4. Season with soy sauce; 5. Stir-fry until cod is fully cooked.

- **Nutritional values:** Calories: 190, Protein: 22g, Carbohydrates: 6g, Fat: 9g, Fiber: 1g.

Spicy Octopus and Snow Pea Stir-Fry

- **Preparation time:** 15 minutes
- **Ingredients:** 1 lb octopus (cut into pieces), 1 cup snow peas, 1 tbsp chili sauce, 1 tsp garlic (minced), 1 tbsp peanut oil.
- **Servings:** 4
- **Cooking method:** Wok Stir-Fry
- **Procedure:** 1. Heat peanut oil, cook garlic in wok; 2. Add octopus, stir-fry briefly; 3. Toss in snow peas and chili sauce; 4. Cook until octopus is tender.
- **Nutritional values:** Calories: 220, Protein: 25g, Carbohydrates: 9g, Fat: 10g, Fiber: 2g.

Honey Mustard Shrimp and Broccoli

- **Preparation time:** 15 minutes
- **Ingredients:** 1 lb shrimp (peeled), 2 cups broccoli florets, 2 tbsp honey, 1 tbsp Dijon mustard, 1 tsp olive oil.
- **Servings:** 4
- **Cooking method:** Wok Stir-Fry
- **Procedure:** 1. Mix honey and mustard; 2. Sauté shrimp in wok with olive oil; 3. Add broccoli; 4. Coat with honey mustard mix; 5. Cook until broccoli is tender.
- **Nutritional values:** Calories: 200, Protein: 24g, Carbohydrates: 13g, Fat: 7g, Fiber: 3g.

Teriyaki Scallop and Mushroom Stir-Fry

- **Preparation time:** 15 minutes
- **Ingredients:** 1 lb scallops, 2 cups mushrooms (sliced), 3 tbsp teriyaki sauce, 1 tsp ginger (minced), 1 tbsp vegetable oil.
- **Servings:** 4
- **Cooking method:** Wok Stir-Fry
- **Procedure:** 1. Heat oil, stir-fry ginger in wok; 2. Add scallops, cook until golden; 3. Introduce mushrooms; 4. Glaze with teriyaki sauce; 5. Stir until mushrooms are soft.
- **Nutritional values:** Calories: 240, Protein: 22g, Carbohydrates: 12g, Fat: 10g, Fiber: 1g.

Vegetarian Stir-Fries

Spicy Tofu and Bell Pepper Stir-Fry

-
- **Preparation time:** 15 minutes
- **Ingredients:** 1 lb firm tofu (cubed), 2 bell peppers (sliced), 1 tbsp chili paste, 2 tbsp soy sauce, 1 tsp sesame oil.
- **Servings:** 4
- **Cooking method:** Wok Stir-Fry
-
-

Procedure: 1. Heat sesame oil in wok; 2. Sauté tofu until golden; 3. Add bell peppers; 4. Stir in chili paste and soy sauce; 5. Cook until peppers are tender.

- **Nutritional values:** Calories: 180, Protein: 12g, Carbohydrates: 8g, Fat: 10g, Fiber: 2g.

Ginger Broccoli and Mushroom Stir-Fry

- **Preparation time:** 15 minutes
- **Ingredients:** 2 cups broccoli florets, 1 cup mushrooms (sliced), 1 tbsp grated ginger, 2 tbsp oyster sauce (vegetarian), 1 tsp vegetable oil.
- **Servings:** 4
- **Cooking method:** Wok Stir-Fry
- **Procedure:** 1. Stir-fry ginger in oil; 2. Add broccoli and mushrooms; 3. Glaze with vegetarian oyster sauce; 4. Cook until broccoli is crisp-tender.
- **Nutritional values:** Calories: 100, Protein: 4g, Carbohydrates: 10g, Fat: 5g, Fiber: 3g.

Sweet and Sour Eggplant

- **Preparation time:** 15 minutes
- **Ingredients:** 2 medium eggplants (cubed), 3 tbsp sweet and sour sauce, 1 red onion (sliced), 1 tbsp soy sauce, 1 tsp sesame seeds.
- **Servings:** 4
- **Cooking method:** Wok Stir-Fry
- **Procedure:** 1. Sauté eggplant and onion in wok; 2. Add sweet and sour sauce and soy sauce; 3. Stir until eggplant is soft; 4. Sprinkle with sesame seeds.
- **Nutritional values:** Calories: 150, Protein: 3g, Carbohydrates: 20g, Fat: 7g, Fiber: 6g.

Thai Basil Tofu Stir-Fry

- **Preparation time:** 15 minutes
- **Ingredients:** 1 lb firm tofu (cubed), 1 cup Thai basil leaves, 2 tbsp soy sauce, 1 chili (sliced), 1 tbsp peanut oil.
- **Servings:** 4
- **Cooking method:** Wok Stir-Fry
- **Procedure:** 1. Heat oil, stir-fry tofu until crisp; 2. Add chili; 3. Stir in basil and soy sauce; 4. Cook until basil wilts.
- **Nutritional values:** Calories: 200, Protein: 12g, Carbohydrates: 6g, Fat: 14g, Fiber: 1g.

Sesame Ginger Carrot Stir-Fry

- **Preparation time:** 15 minutes
- **Ingredients:** 3 carrots (julienned), 2 tbsp sesame oil, 1 tbsp minced ginger, 1 tbsp soy sauce, 1 tsp sesame seeds.
- **Servings:** 4
- **Cooking method:** Wok Stir-Fry
- **Procedure:** 1. Heat sesame oil; 2. Add ginger and carrots; 3. Season with soy sauce; 4. Stir-fry until tender; 5. Garnish with sesame seeds.
- **Nutritional values:** Calories: 120, Protein: 2g, Carbohydrates: 10g, Fat: 8g, Fiber: 3g.

Spicy Garlic Bok Choy

- **Preparation time:** 15 minutes
- **Ingredients:** 4 cups baby bok choy, 2 garlic cloves (minced), 1 tbsp chili oil, 1 tsp soy sauce, 1 tsp crushed red pepper flakes.
- **Servings:** 4
- **Cooking method:** Wok Stir-Fry
- **Procedure:** 1. Stir-fry garlic in chili oil; 2. Add bok choy; 3. Season with soy sauce and red pepper; 4. Cook until bok choy is wilted.
- **Nutritional values:** Calories: 80, Protein: 3g, Carbohydrates: 6g, Fat: 5g, Fiber: 2g.

Mixed Pepper and Cashew Stir-Fry

- **Preparation time:** 15 minutes
- **Ingredients:** 1 cup bell peppers (mixed colors, sliced), 1/2 cup cashews, 2 tbsp hoisin sauce, 1 tsp ginger (minced), 1 tbsp canola oil.
- **Servings:** 4
- **Cooking method:** Wok Stir-Fry

- **Procedure:** 1. Heat oil, stir-fry ginger; 2. Add bell peppers; 3. Stir in cashews and hoisin sauce; 4. Cook until peppers are soft.
- **Nutritional values:** Calories: 180, Protein: 5g, Carbohydrates: 12g, Fat: 13g, Fiber: 2g.

Zucchini and Yellow Squash Stir-Fry

- **Preparation time:** 15 minutes
- **Ingredients:** 2 zucchinis (sliced), 2 yellow squashes (sliced), 1 tbsp soy sauce, 1 tsp garlic (minced), 1 tbsp olive oil.
- **Servings:** 4
- **Cooking method:** Wok Stir-Fry
- **Procedure:** 1. Heat olive oil, sauté garlic; 2. Add zucchini and squash; 3. Season with soy sauce; 4. Cook until vegetables are tender but crisp.
- **Nutritional values:** Calories: 100, Protein: 3g, Carbohydrates: 8g, Fat: 7g, Fiber: 3g.

Tofu and Tempeh Stir-Fries

Crispy Tofu with Sweet Chili Sauce

- **Preparation time:** 15 minutes

- **Ingredients:** 1 lb firm tofu (cubed), 2 tbsp sweet chili sauce, 1 red bell pepper (sliced), 1 tbsp cornstarch, 2 tsp sesame oil.
- **Servings:** 4

- **Cooking method:** Wok Stir-Fry
- **Procedure:** 1. Toss tofu in cornstarch; 2. Fry tofu in wok with sesame oil until crispy; 3. Add bell pepper; 4. Glaze with sweet chili sauce.
- **Nutritional values:** Calories: 190, Protein: 12g, Carbohydrates: 15g, Fat: 9g, Fiber: 2g.

Tempeh and Broccoli in Garlic Sauce

- **Preparation time:** 15 minutes
- **Ingredients:** 1 lb tempeh (cubed), 2 cups broccoli florets, 2 garlic cloves (minced), 2 tbsp soy sauce, 1 tsp vegetable oil.
- **Servings:** 4
- **Cooking method:** Wok Stir-Fry
- **Procedure:** 1. Sauté garlic and tempeh in oil; 2. Add broccoli; 3. Season with soy sauce; 4. Stir-fry until tempeh is golden and broccoli is tender.
- **Nutritional values:** Calories: 250, Protein: 18g, Carbohydrates: 15g, Fat: 14g, Fiber: 5g.

Spicy Orange Tofu Stir-Fry

- **Preparation time:** 15 minutes
- **Ingredients:** 1 lb firm tofu (cubed), Juice of 1 orange, 1 tbsp chili flakes, 1 green bell pepper (sliced), 1 tbsp olive oil.
- **Servings:** 4
- **Cooking method:** Wok Stir-Fry
- **Procedure:** 1. Cook tofu in olive oil until crisp; 2. Add bell pepper; 3. Pour orange juice; 4. Season with chili flakes; 5. Cook until sauce thickens.
- **Nutritional values:** Calories: 200, Protein: 12g, Carbohydrates: 10g, Fat: 12g, Fiber: 3g.

Tempeh with Cashew and Peas

- **Preparation time:** 15 minutes
- **Ingredients:** 1 lb tempeh (sliced), 1/2 cup cashews, 1 cup peas, 2 tbsp hoisin sauce, 1 tsp sesame oil.
- **Servings:** 4
- **Cooking method:** Wok Stir-Fry
- **Procedure:** 1. Heat sesame oil, brown tempeh; 2. Add cashews and peas; 3. Glaze with hoisin sauce; 4. Stir until well mixed.
- **Nutritional values:** Calories: 300, Protein: 20g, Carbohydrates: 18g, Fat: 18g, Fiber: 5g.

Szechuan Tofu with Bell Peppers

- **Preparation time:** 15 minutes
- **Ingredients:** 1 lb firm tofu (cubed), 2 bell peppers (mixed colors, sliced), 1 tbsp Szechuan sauce, 1 tsp ginger (minced), 1 tbsp canola oil.
- **Servings:** 4
- **Cooking method:** Wok Stir-Fry
- **Procedure:** 1. Stir-fry ginger in oil; 2. Add tofu and bell peppers; 3. Toss with Szechuan sauce; 4. Cook until peppers are tender and tofu is coated.
- **Nutritional values:** Calories: 220, Protein: 12g, Carbohydrates: 10g, Fat: 14g, Fiber: 3g.

Teriyaki Tempeh with Green Beans

- **Preparation time:** 15 minutes
- **Ingredients:** 1 lb tempeh (cubed), 2 cups green beans (trimmed), 3 tbsp teriyaki sauce, 1 tsp garlic (minced), 1 tbsp olive oil.
- **Servings:** 4
- **Cooking method:** Wok Stir-Fry
- **Procedure:** 1. Sauté garlic in olive oil; 2. Add tempeh, brown slightly; 3. Introduce green beans; 4. Glaze with teriyaki sauce; 5. Stir-fry until beans are crisp.

- **Nutritional values:** Calories: 280, Protein: 19g, Carbohydrates: 20g, Fat: 16g, Fiber: 6g.

Lemon Pepper Tofu with Asparagus

- **Preparation time:** 15 minutes
- **Ingredients:** 1 lb firm tofu (cubed), 2 cups asparagus (chopped), 1 tbsp lemon pepper seasoning, 1 lemon (juice), 1 tbsp grapeseed oil.
- **Servings:** 4
- **Cooking method:** Wok Stir-Fry
- **Procedure:** 1. Season tofu with lemon pepper; 2. Stir-fry in grapeseed oil; 3. Add asparagus; 4. Drizzle with lemon juice; 5. Cook until asparagus is tender.
- **Nutritional values:** Calories: 180, Protein: 12g, Carbohydrates: 8g, Fat: 12g, Fiber: 4g.

Maple Glazed Tempeh with Carrots

- **Preparation time:** 15 minutes
- **Ingredients:** 1 lb tempeh (sliced), 2 carrots (julienned), 2 tbsp maple syrup, 1 tbsp soy sauce, 1 tsp sesame oil.
- **Servings:** 4
- **Cooking method:** Wok Stir-Fry

- **Procedure:** 1. Heat sesame oil; 2. Cook tempeh until golden; 3. Add carrots; 4. Blend in maple syrup and soy sauce; 5. Cook until carrots are tender.
- **Nutritional values:** Calories: 260, Protein: 18g, Carbohydrates: 20g, Fat: 14g, Fiber: 5g.

Chapter IV: Steamy Affairs

Steamed Fish Delights

Ginger Soy Steamed Salmon

- **Preparation time:** 15 minutes
- **Ingredients:** 4 salmon fillets, 2 tbsp soy sauce, 1 tbsp grated ginger, 1 green onion (sliced), 1 tsp sesame oil.
- **Servings:** 4
- **Cooking method:** Wok Steaming
-
-

- **Procedure:** 1. Place salmon in steaming basket; 2. Drizzle with soy sauce and sesame oil; 3. Top with ginger and green onion; 4. Steam in wok until cooked through.
- **Nutritional values:** Calories: 250, Protein: 23g, Carbohydrates: 2g, Fat: 17g, Fiber: 0g.

Lemon Herb Steamed Cod

- **Preparation time:** 15 minutes
- **Ingredients:** 4 cod fillets, Juice of 1 lemon, 1 tbsp chopped dill, 1 tbsp chopped parsley, 1 tsp olive oil.
- **Servings:** 4
- **Cooking method:** Wok Steaming
- **Procedure:** 1. Rub cod with olive oil and herbs; 2. Place in steaming basket; 3. Squeeze lemon juice over cod; 4. Steam in wok until flaky.
- **Nutritional values:** Calories: 190, Protein: 20g, Carbohydrates: 1g, Fat: 11g, Fiber: 0g.

Spicy Garlic Steamed Tilapia

- **Preparation time:** 15 minutes
- **Ingredients:** 4 tilapia fillets, 2 garlic cloves (minced), 1 tsp chili flakes, 2 tbsp lime juice, 1 tsp vegetable oil.
- **Servings:** 4
- **Cooking method:** Wok Steaming
- **Procedure:** 1. Marinate tilapia in lime juice, garlic, and chili; 2. Oil the steaming basket; 3. Place fish in basket; 4. Steam in wok until tender.
- **Nutritional values:** Calories: 180, Protein: 34g, Carbohydrates: 2g, Fat: 3g, Fiber: 0.5g.

Soy Glazed Steamed Trout

- **Preparation time:** 15 minutes
- **Ingredients:** 4 trout fillets, 2 tbsp soy sauce, 1 tsp honey, 1 tsp minced ginger, 1 green onion (chopped).
- **Servings:** 4
- **Cooking method:** Wok Steaming
- **Procedure:** 1. Mix soy sauce, honey, and ginger; 2. Brush mixture on trout; 3. Place in steaming basket; 4. Garnish with green onion; 5. Steam in wok until done.
- **Nutritional values:** Calories: 210, Protein: 25g, Carbohydrates: 5g, Fat: 10g, Fiber: 0g.

Steamed Snapper with Lime and Cilantro

- **Preparation time:** 15 minutes
- **Ingredients:** 4 snapper fillets, Juice of 2 limes, 1 tbsp chopped cilantro, 1 tsp minced garlic, 1 tsp olive oil.
- **Servings:** 4
- **Cooking method:** Wok Steaming
- **Procedure:** 1. Combine lime juice, garlic, cilantro; 2. Brush on snapper; 3. Oil the steaming basket; 4. Place fish in basket; 5. Steam in wok until cooked.
- **Nutritional values:** Calories: 200, Protein: 35g, Carbohydrates: 1g, Fat: 5g, Fiber: 0g.

Asian Steamed Halibut

- **Preparation time:** 15 minutes
- **Ingredients:** 4 halibut fillets, 2 tbsp teriyaki sauce, 1 tsp sesame seeds, 1 green onion (sliced), 1 tsp grated ginger.
- **Servings:** 4
- **Cooking method:** Wok Steaming
- **Procedure:** 1. Rub halibut with ginger and teriyaki; 2. Sprinkle sesame seeds; 3. Place in steaming basket; 4. Top with green onion; 5. Steam in wok until opaque.
- **Nutritional values:** Calories: 220, Protein: 32g, Carbohydrates: 3g, Fat: 8g, Fiber: 0.5g.

Herbed Steamed Mahi Mahi

- **Preparation time:** 15 minutes
- **Ingredients:** 4 mahi mahi fillets, 1 tbsp mixed herbs (thyme, oregano, basil), 1 lemon (sliced), 1 tsp olive oil, Salt and pepper to taste.
- **Servings:** 4
- **Cooking method:** Wok Steaming
- **Procedure:** 1. Season fish with herbs, salt, and pepper; 2. Drizzle with olive oil; 3. Place lemon slices on fillets; 4. Steam in wok until fish flakes easily.

- **Nutritional values:** Calories: 210, Protein: 30g, Carbohydrates: 1g, Fat: 9g, Fiber: 0g.

Balsamic Glazed Steamed Bass

- **Preparation time:** 15 minutes
- **Ingredients:** 4 bass fillets, 2 tbsp balsamic vinegar, 1 tsp honey, 1 tsp Dijon mustard, 1 tsp olive oil.
- **Servings:** 4
- **Cooking method:** Wok Steaming
- **Procedure:** 1. Whisk together balsamic, honey, mustard; 2. Brush on bass; 3. Oil steaming basket; 4. Steam bass in wok; 5. Cook until done.
- **Nutritional values:** Calories: 220, Protein: 24g, Carbohydrates: 4g, Fat: 12g, Fiber: 0g.

Steamed Vegetable Medleys

Ginger Soy Steamed Broccoli and Carrots

- **Preparation time:** 15 minutes
- **Ingredients:** 2 cups broccoli florets, 2 carrots (sliced), 1 tbsp soy sauce, 1 tsp grated ginger, 1 tsp sesame oil.
- **Servings:** 4
- **Cooking method:** Wok Steaming
- **Procedure:** 1. Place broccoli and carrots in steaming basket; 2. Drizzle with soy sauce and sesame oil; 3. Top with grated ginger; 4. Steam in wok until vegetables are tender.
- **Nutritional values:** Calories: 70, Protein: 3g, Carbohydrates: 10g, Fat: 2g, Fiber: 4g.

Lemon Garlic Steamed Asparagus and Peppers

- **Preparation time:** 15 minutes
- **Ingredients:** 1 bunch asparagus (trimmed), 1 red bell pepper (sliced), 2 garlic cloves (minced), Juice of 1 lemon, 1 tsp olive oil.
- **Servings:** 4
- **Cooking method:** Wok Steaming
- **Procedure:** 1. Combine asparagus and bell pepper in steaming basket; 2. Mix lemon juice, garlic, and olive oil; 3. Drizzle over vegetables; 4. Steam in wok until crisp-tender.
- **Nutritional values:** Calories: 60, Protein: 3g, Carbohydrates: 8g, Fat: 2g, Fiber: 3g.

Spiced Cauliflower and Green Bean Medley

- **Preparation time:** 15 minutes
- **Ingredients:** 2 cups cauliflower florets, 1 cup green beans, 1 tsp curry powder, 1 tsp cumin, 1 tsp olive oil.
- **Servings:** 4
- **Cooking method:** Wok Steaming
- **Procedure:** 1. Toss cauliflower and green beans with spices and oil; 2. Place in steaming basket; 3. Steam in wok until vegetables are tender.
- **Nutritional values:** Calories: 50, Protein: 2g, Carbohydrates: 8g, Fat: 2g, Fiber: 3g.

Balsamic Glazed Steamed Zucchini and Squash

- **Preparation time:** 15 minutes
- **Ingredients:** 2 zucchinis (sliced), 2 yellow squashes (sliced), 2 tbsp balsamic vinegar, 1 tsp honey, 1 tsp olive oil.
- **Servings:** 4
- **Cooking method:** Wok Steaming
- **Procedure:** 1. Arrange zucchini and squash in steaming basket; 2. Whisk together balsamic vinegar, honey, and oil; 3. Drizzle over vegetables; 4. Steam in wok until tender.
- **Nutritional values:** Calories: 80, Protein: 2g, Carbohydrates: 12g, Fat: 3g, Fiber: 3g.

Soy Ginger Steamed Mixed Vegetables

- **Preparation time:** 15 minutes
- **Ingredients:** 1 cup broccoli florets, 1 cup sliced mushrooms, 1 carrot (sliced), 1 tbsp soy sauce, 1 tsp grated ginger.
- **Servings:** 4
- **Cooking method:** Wok Steaming
- **Procedure:** 1. Combine vegetables in steaming basket; 2. Mix soy sauce and ginger; 3. Drizzle over vegetables; 4. Steam in wok until all vegetables are tender.

- **Nutritional values:** Calories: 60, Protein: 4g, Carbohydrates: 10g, Fat: 1g, Fiber: 3g.

Garlic Lemon Steamed Brussels Sprouts and Bell Peppers

- **Preparation time:** 15 minutes
- **Ingredients:** 2 cups Brussels sprouts (halved), 1 bell pepper (sliced), 2 garlic cloves (minced), Juice of 1 lemon, 1 tsp olive oil.
- **Servings:** 4
- **Cooking method:** Wok Steaming
- **Procedure:** 1. Mix Brussels sprouts and bell pepper in steaming basket; 2. Combine garlic, lemon juice, and oil; 3. Drizzle mixture over vegetables; 4. Steam in wok until sprouts are tender.
- **Nutritional values:** Calories: 70, Protein: 3g, Carbohydrates: 10g, Fat: 2g, Fiber: 4g.

Sweet Chili Steamed Snow Peas and Carrots

- **Preparation time:** 15 minutes
- **Ingredients:** 2 cups snow peas, 2 carrots (julienned), 2 tbsp sweet chili sauce, 1 tsp sesame seeds, 1 tsp sesame oil.
- **Servings:** 4
- **Cooking method:** Wok Steaming

- **Procedure:** 1. Place snow peas and carrots in steaming basket; 2. Drizzle with sweet chili sauce and sesame oil; 3. Top with sesame seeds; 4. Steam in wok until veggies are crisp-tender.
- **Nutritional values:** Calories: 80, Protein: 2g, Carbohydrates: 12g, Fat: 3g, Fiber: 3g.

Herbed Steamed Artichokes and Cherry Tomatoes

- **Preparation time:** 15 minutes
- **Ingredients:** 4 baby artichokes (halved), 1 cup cherry tomatoes, 1 tbsp mixed herbs (thyme, basil), 1 tsp olive oil, Salt and pepper to taste.

- **Servings:** 4
- **Cooking method:** Wok Steaming
- **Procedure:** 1. Season artichokes and tomatoes with herbs, salt, and pepper; 2. Drizzle with olive oil; 3. Place in steaming basket; 4. Steam in wok until artichokes are tender.
- **Nutritional values:** Calories: 90, Protein: 3g, Carbohydrates: 13g, Fat: 4g, Fiber: 5g.

Dim Sum Favorites

Classic Shrimp Dumplings (Har Gow)

- **Preparation time:** 20 minutes
- **Ingredients:** 1/2 lb shrimp (minced), 1 tbsp bamboo shoots (finely chopped), 1 tsp sesame oil, Dumpling wrappers, 1 tsp soy sauce.
- **Servings:** 4
- **Cooking method:** Wok Steaming

- **Procedure:** 1. Combine shrimp, bamboo shoots, sesame oil, and soy sauce; 2. Place mixture in wrappers, seal edges; 3. Steam in wok until translucent.
- **Nutritional values:** Calories: 150, Protein: 15g, Carbohydrates: 15g, Fat: 3g, Fiber: 1g.

Vegetarian Steamed Buns (Baozi)

- **Preparation time:** 30 minutes (includes dough rising time)
- **Ingredients:** 2 cups all-purpose flour, 1/2 cup warm water, 1 tsp yeast, 1 cup mixed vegetables (finely chopped), 1 tbsp hoisin sauce.
- **Servings:** 4
- **Cooking method:** Wok Steaming

- **Procedure:** 1. Mix flour, water, yeast to form dough, let rise; 2. Sauté vegetables with hoisin sauce; 3. Fill dough with mixture, form buns; 4. Steam buns in wok until puffy.
- **Nutritional values:** Calories: 220, Protein: 6g, Carbohydrates: 45g, Fat: 1g, Fiber: 3g.

Pork Siu Mai

- **Preparation time:** 20 minutes
- **Ingredients:** 1/2 lb ground pork, 1/4 lb shrimp (minced), 1 tsp soy sauce, Siu Mai wrappers, 1 tsp sesame oil.
- **Servings:** 4
- **Cooking method:** Wok Steaming

- **Procedure:** 1. Mix pork, shrimp, soy sauce, and sesame oil; 2. Place mixture in Siu Mai wrappers, leave top open; 3. Steam in wok until cooked.
- **Nutritional values:** Calories: 200, Protein: 20g, Carbohydrates: 15g, Fat: 7g, Fiber: 1g.

Chicken and Mushroom Steamed Rolls

- **Preparation time:** 20 minutes
- **Ingredients:** 1/2 lb chicken (minced), 1 cup mushrooms (finely chopped), 1 tbsp oyster sauce, Spring roll wrappers, 1 tsp ginger (minced).
- **Servings:** 4
- **Cooking method:** Wok Steaming
- **Procedure:** 1. Combine chicken, mushrooms, ginger, and oyster sauce; 2. Roll in wrappers; 3. Steam rolls in wok until filling is cooked.
- **Nutritional values:** Calories: 180, Protein: 15g, Carbohydrates: 20g, Fat: 5g, Fiber: 2g.

Steamed Beef Meatballs

- **Preparation time:** 20 minutes
- **Ingredients:** 1/2 lb ground beef, 1 tbsp soy sauce, 1 tsp cornstarch, 1 green onion (chopped), 1 tsp ginger (minced).
- **Servings:** 4
- **Cooking method:** Wok Steaming
- **Procedure:** 1. Mix beef, soy sauce, cornstarch, ginger; 2. Form into small meatballs; 3. Steam in wok until cooked through; 4. Garnish with green onion.
- **Nutritional values:** Calories: 160, Protein: 15g, Carbohydrates: 3g, Fat: 9g, Fiber: 0g.

Tofu and Vegetable Dumplings

- **Preparation time:** 20 minutes
- **Ingredients:** 1/2 lb firm tofu (crumbled), 1 cup mixed vegetables (finely chopped), Dumpling wrappers, 1 tbsp soy sauce, 1 tsp sesame oil.
- **Servings:** 4
- **Cooking method:** Wok Steaming
- **Procedure:** 1. Combine tofu, vegetables, soy sauce, and oil; 2. Fill and seal dumpling wrappers; 3. Steam in wok until wrappers are tender.

- **Nutritional values:** Calories: 150, Protein: 9g, Carbohydrates: 20g, Fat: 4g, Fiber: 2g.

Lotus Leaf Wrapped Sticky Rice

- **Preparation time:** 30 minutes
- **Ingredients:** 2 cups sticky rice (soaked), 1/2 cup chicken (diced), 1/4 cup mushrooms (diced), 2 lotus leaves (soaked), 1 tbsp soy sauce.
- **Servings:** 4
- **Cooking method:** Wok Steaming
- **Procedure:** 1. Mix rice, chicken, mushrooms, soy sauce; 2. Divide mixture onto lotus leaves; 3. Wrap and steam in wok until rice is cooked.
- **Nutritional values:** Calories: 300, Protein: 10g, Carbohydrates: 55g, Fat: 3g, Fiber: 2g.

Cheung Fun (Rice Noodle Rolls)

- **Preparation time:** 25 minutes
- **Ingredients:** 1 cup rice flour, 2 cups water, 1 tbsp vegetable oil, 1/2 cup shrimp (chopped), 1 tbsp light soy sauce.
- **Servings:** 4
- **Cooking method:** Wok Steaming

- **Procedure:** 1. Mix rice flour with water; 2. Pour thin layer into oiled tray; 3. Add shrimp on top; 4. Steam in wok until set; 5. Roll and drizzle with soy sauce.
- **Nutritional values:** Calories: 200, Protein: 8g, Carbohydrates: 35g, Fat: 3g, Fiber: 1g.

Steamed Rice and Noodles

Classic Steamed Jasmine Rice

- **Preparation time:** 18 minutes
- **Ingredients:** 2 cups jasmine rice, 3 cups water, 1 tsp salt.
- **Servings:** 4
- **Cooking method:** Wok Steaming
- **Procedure:** 1. Rinse rice until water runs clear; 2. Combine rice, water, and salt in heatproof dish; 3. Steam in wok covered for 18 minutes.
- **Nutritional values:** Calories: 205, Protein: 4g, Carbohydrates: 45g, Fat: 0g, Fiber: 1g.

Ginger Scallion Steamed Noodles

- **Preparation time:** 20 minutes
- **Ingredients:** 8 oz rice noodles, 2 tbsp soy sauce, 1 tbsp grated ginger, 2 green onions (sliced), 1 tsp sesame oil.
- **Servings:** 4
- **Cooking method:** Wok Steaming
- **Procedure:** 1. Soak noodles until soft; 2. Mix soy sauce, ginger, and sesame oil; 3. Toss noodles with sauce and green onions; 4. Steam in wok until heated through.
- **Nutritional values:** Calories: 220, Protein: 4g, Carbohydrates: 42g, Fat: 4g, Fiber: 2g.

Steamed Coconut Rice

- **Preparation time:** 20 minutes
- **Ingredients:** 2 cups basmati rice, 1 can coconut milk, 1/2 cup water, 1 tsp salt, 1 bay leaf.
- **Servings:** 4
- **Cooking method:** Wok Steaming
- **Procedure:** 1. Rinse rice thoroughly; 2. Mix rice with coconut milk, water, salt, and bay leaf; 3. Steam in wok covered until fluffy.
- **Nutritional values:** Calories: 300, Protein: 5g, Carbohydrates: 50g, Fat: 10g, Fiber: 1g.

Steamed Soba Noodles with Vegetables

- **Preparation time:** 15 minutes
- **Ingredients:** 8 oz soba noodles, 1 cup mixed vegetables (julienned), 2 tbsp teriyaki sauce, 1 tsp sesame seeds, 1 tsp sesame oil.
- **Servings:** 4
- **Cooking method:** Wok Steaming
- **Procedure:** 1. Cook soba noodles, rinse cold; 2. Toss noodles with vegetables, teriyaki sauce, and sesame oil; 3. Steam in wok until heated; 4. Garnish with sesame seeds.
- **Nutritional values:** Calories: 230, Protein: 8g, Carbohydrates: 42g, Fat: 4g, Fiber: 3g.
  -

Steamed Brown Rice with Herbs

- **Preparation time:** 30 minutes
- **Ingredients:** 2 cups brown rice, 3 1/4 cups water, 1 tbsp mixed herbs (chopped), 1 tsp olive oil, Salt to taste.
- **Servings:** 4
- **Cooking method:** Wok Steaming
- **Procedure:** 1. Rinse rice thoroughly; 2. Mix rice with water, olive oil, herbs, and salt; 3. Steam in wok covered until tender.

- **Nutritional values:** Calories: 215, Protein: 5g, Carbohydrates: 45g, Fat: 2g, Fiber: 3g.

Steamed Vermicelli with Soy Ginger Sauce

- **Preparation time:** 15 minutes
- **Ingredients:** 8 oz rice vermicelli, 2 tbsp soy sauce, 1 tbsp grated ginger, 1 tbsp rice vinegar, 1 tsp sugar.
- **Servings:** 4
- **Cooking method:** Wok Steaming
- **Procedure:** 1. Soak vermicelli until soft; 2. Mix soy sauce, ginger, vinegar, and sugar; 3. Toss noodles with sauce; 4. Steam in wok until warm.
- **Nutritional values:** Calories: 210, Protein: 2g, Carbohydrates: 46g, Fat: 1g, Fiber: 2g.

Lemon Grass Steamed Rice

- **Preparation time:** 20 minutes
- **Ingredients:** 2 cups sticky rice, 1 stalk lemongrass (minced), 2 1/2 cups water, 1 lime (zest), Salt to taste.
- **Servings:** 4
- **Cooking method:** Wok Steaming
- **Procedure:** 1. Soak rice for 1 hour, rinse; 2. Mix rice with water, lemongrass, lime zest, and salt; 3. Steam in wok until sticky and tender.

- **Nutritional values:** Calories: 230, Protein: 4g, Carbohydrates: 51g, Fat: 1g, Fiber: 2g.

Steamed Udon with Mushroom Sauce

- **Preparation time:** 20 minutes
- **Ingredients:** 8 oz udon noodles, 1 cup mushrooms (sliced), 2 tbsp oyster sauce, 1 tsp garlic (minced), 1 tsp sesame oil.
- **Servings:** 4
- **Cooking method:** Wok Steaming
- **Procedure:** 1. Cook udon noodles, rinse cold; 2. Sauté mushrooms, garlic; 3. Mix with oyster sauce and sesame oil; 4. Toss with noodles; 5. Steam in wok until hot.
- **Nutritional values:** Calories: 250, Protein: 10g, Carbohydrates: 50g, Fat: 3g, Fiber: 3g.

Chapter V: Savor the Flavor

Soups and Broths

Wok-Simmered Chicken Noodle Soup

- **Preparation time:** 25 minutes
- **Ingredients:** 1 lb chicken breast, 6 cups chicken broth, 2 carrots (sliced), 2 celery stalks (sliced), 8 oz egg noodles, 1 tsp thyme.
- **Servings:** 4
- **Cooking method:** Wok Simmering
- **Procedure:** 1. Add chicken, broth to wok; 2. Bring to boil, simmer until chicken cooked; 3. Shred chicken, return to broth; 4. Add vegetables, noodles, thyme; 5. Simmer until noodles are tender.
- **Nutritional values:** Calories: 350, Protein: 25g, Carbohydrates: 40g, Fat: 10g, Fiber: 3g.

Spicy Wok-Tom Yum Soup

- **Preparation time:** 20 minutes
- **Ingredients:** 4 cups vegetable broth, 1 lemongrass stalk, 1-inch piece galangal (sliced), 2 kaffir lime leaves, 1 cup mushrooms (sliced), 1 tbsp fish sauce, 1 tsp chili paste, Juice of 1 lime.
- **Servings:** 4
- **Cooking method:** Wok Simmering
- **Procedure:** 1. Boil broth with lemongrass, galangal, lime leaves in wok; 2. Add mushrooms, simmer 10 mins; 3. Stir in fish sauce, chili paste, lime juice.
- **Nutritional values:** Calories: 60, Protein: 2g, Carbohydrates: 10g, Fat: 1g, Fiber: 1g.

Wok-Hearty Beef and Vegetable Soup

- **Preparation time:** 30 minutes
- **Ingredients:** 1 lb beef stew meat, 6 cups beef broth, 2 potatoes (cubed), 1 onion (chopped), 2 carrots (sliced), 1 tsp rosemary.
- **Servings:** 4
- **Cooking method:** Wok Simmering
- **Procedure:** 1. Brown beef in wok; 2. Add broth, vegetables, rosemary; 3. Simmer until beef is tender and veggies are cooked.

- **Nutritional values:** Calories: 300, Protein: 25g, Carbohydrates: 25g, Fat: 12g, Fiber: 4g.

Wok-Simmered Miso Soup with Tofu

- **Preparation time:** 15 minutes
- **Ingredients:** 4 cups dashi stock, 3 tbsp miso paste, 1 block silken tofu (cubed), 1 cup seaweed (wakame), 2 green onions (sliced).
- **Servings:** 4
- **Cooking method:** Wok Simmering
- **Procedure:** 1. Heat dashi in wok, don't boil; 2. Dissolve miso paste in stock; 3. Add tofu, seaweed; 4. Heat gently, garnish with green onions.
- **Nutritional values:** Calories: 120, Protein: 8g, Carbohydrates: 10g, Fat: 5g, Fiber: 2g.

Spicy Wok Hot and Sour Soup

- **Preparation time:** 20 minutes
- **Ingredients:** 4 cups chicken broth, 1 tbsp soy sauce, 2 tbsp rice vinegar, 1 tsp chili oil, 1 cup mushrooms (sliced), 1 egg (beaten), 1 tbsp cornstarch (mixed with water).
- **Servings:** 4
- **Cooking method:** Wok Simmering

- **Procedure:** 1. Combine broth, soy sauce, vinegar, chili oil in wok; 2. Add mushrooms, simmer 10 mins; 3. Drizzle in egg, stir; 4. Thicken with cornstarch mix.
- **Nutritional values:** Calories: 80, Protein: 4g, Carbohydrates: 8g, Fat: 4g, Fiber: 1g.

Wok-Cooked Vegetable Broth with Noodles

- **Preparation time:** 20 minutes
- **Ingredients:** 4 cups vegetable broth, 2 cups mixed vegetables (carrots, peas, corn), 8 oz rice noodles, 1 tbsp soy sauce, 1 tsp ginger (minced).
- **Servings:** 4
- **Cooking method:** Wok Simmering
- **Procedure:** 1. Bring broth to simmer in wok; 2. Add vegetables, cook until tender; 3. Add noodles, soy sauce, ginger; 4. Cook until noodles are soft.
- **Nutritional values:** Calories: 220, Protein: 4g, Carbohydrates: 48g, Fat: 1g, Fiber: 3g.

Simple Wok Chicken Broth

- **Preparation time:** 25 minutes
- **Ingredients:** 1 chicken carcass, 6 cups water, 1 onion (halved), 2 carrots (chopped), 2 celery stalks (chopped), 1 bay leaf, Salt and pepper to taste.
- **Servings:** 4
- **Cooking method:** Wok Simmering
- **Procedure:** 1. Place all ingredients in wok; 2. Bring to boil, reduce to simmer for 25 mins; 3. Strain, season with salt and pepper.
- **Nutritional values:** Calories: 40, Protein: 3g, Carbohydrates: 5g, Fat: 1g, Fiber: 1g.

Wok-Warmed Tomato and Basil Soup

- **Preparation time:** 20 minutes
- **Ingredients:** 4 cups tomato juice, 1 cup diced tomatoes, 1 tsp sugar, 1 tbsp fresh basil (chopped), Salt and pepper to taste, 1 tbsp olive oil.
- **Servings:** 4
- **Cooking method:** Wok Simmering
- **Procedure:** 1. Heat olive oil in wok; 2. Add tomato juice, diced tomatoes, sugar; 3. Simmer 15 mins; 4. Season with basil, salt, and pepper.
- **Nutritional values:** Calories: 80, Protein: 2g, Carbohydrates: 12g, Fat: 3g, Fiber: 2g.

Curries and Stews

Classic Chicken Curry

- **Preparation time:** 30 minutes
- **Ingredients:** 1 lb chicken (cubed), 1 onion (chopped), 2 tomatoes (chopped), 2 tbsp curry powder, 1 cup coconut milk, 1 tsp ginger (minced), 2 garlic cloves (minced), 2 tbsp vegetable oil.
- **Servings:** 4
- **Cooking method:** Wok Cooking

- **Procedure:** 1. Sauté onion, ginger, garlic in oil; 2. Add chicken, brown lightly; 3. Stir in curry powder; 4. Add tomatoes, coconut milk; 5. Simmer until chicken is cooked.
- **Nutritional values:** Calories: 350, Protein: 25g, Carbohydrates: 10g, Fat: 25g, Fiber: 3g.

Beef and Potato Stew

- **Preparation time:** 40 minutes
- **Ingredients:** 1 lb beef stew meat, 3 potatoes (cubed), 1 onion (chopped), 2 carrots (sliced), 4 cups beef broth, 1 tsp thyme, 2 tbsp olive oil.
- **Servings:** 4
- **Cooking method:** Wok Cooking
- **Procedure:** 1. Brown beef in oil; 2. Add onions, carrots; 3. Pour in broth; 4. Add potatoes, thyme; 5. Simmer until meat is tender.
- **Nutritional values:** Calories: 450, Protein: 30g, Carbohydrates: 40g, Fat: 20g, Fiber: 5g.

Thai Green Curry with Vegetables

- **Preparation time:** 25 minutes
- **Ingredients:** 2 cups mixed vegetables (bell peppers, zucchini, peas), 1 can green curry paste, 1 can coconut milk, 1 tbsp fish sauce, 1 tsp sugar, 1 tbsp vegetable oil.
- **Servings:** 4
- **Cooking method:** Wok Cooking
- **Procedure:** 1. Sauté vegetables in oil; 2. Stir in curry paste; 3. Add coconut milk, fish sauce, sugar; 4. Simmer until vegetables are tender.

- **Nutritional values:** Calories: 300, Protein: 5g, Carbohydrates: 15g, Fat: 25g, Fiber: 4g.

Wok-Simmered Lamb Stew

- **Preparation time:** 40 minutes
- **Ingredients:** 1 lb lamb (cubed), 1 onion (chopped), 2 cups chicken broth, 1 cup diced tomatoes, 2 carrots (sliced), 1 tsp rosemary, 2 tbsp olive oil.
- **Servings:** 4
- **Cooking method:** Wok Cooking
- **Procedure:** 1. Brown lamb in oil; 2. Add onions, carrots; 3. Pour in broth, tomatoes; 4. Season with rosemary; 5. Simmer until lamb is tender.
- **Nutritional values:** Calories: 400, Protein: 30g, Carbohydrates: 20g, Fat: 25g, Fiber: 4g.

Coconut Shrimp Curry

- **Preparation time:** 30 minutes
- **Ingredients:** 1 lb shrimp (peeled), 1 onion (chopped), 1 can coconut milk, 2 tbsp curry powder, 1 red bell pepper (sliced), 1 tsp ginger (minced), 1 tsp garlic (minced), 2 tbsp vegetable oil.
- **Servings:** 4
- **Cooking method:** Wok Cooking

- **Procedure:** 1. Sauté onion, ginger, garlic in oil; 2. Add bell pepper, cook slightly; 3. Stir in curry powder; 4. Add shrimp, coconut milk; 5. Simmer until shrimp is cooked.
- **Nutritional values:** Calories: 350, Protein: 25g, Carbohydrates: 15g, Fat: 20g, Fiber: 2g.

Vegetarian Chickpea Curry

- **Preparation time:** 25 minutes
- **Ingredients:** 2 cans chickpeas (drained), 1 onion (chopped), 2 tomatoes (chopped), 1 can coconut milk, 2 tbsp curry powder, 1 tsp cumin, 1 tbsp olive oil.
- **Servings:** 4
- **Cooking method:** Wok Cooking
- **Procedure:** 1. Sauté onion in oil; 2. Add tomatoes, cook until soft; 3. Stir in chickpeas, curry powder, cumin; 4. Pour in coconut milk; 5. Simmer for 15 minutes.
- **Nutritional values:** Calories: 350, Protein: 10g, Carbohydrates: 40g, Fat: 18g, Fiber: 10g.

Wok-Cooked Spicy Lentil Stew

- **Preparation time:** 30 minutes
- **Ingredients:** 2 cups lentils, 1 onion (chopped), 1 carrot (sliced), 4 cups vegetable broth, 1 tsp chili powder, 1 tsp cumin, 2 tbsp olive oil.
- **Servings:** 4
- **Cooking method:** Wok Cooking
- **Procedure:** 1. Sauté onion, carrot in oil; 2. Add lentils, broth; 3. Season with chili powder, cumin; 4. Simmer until lentils are tender.
- **Nutritional values:** Calories: 300, Protein: 18g, Carbohydrates: 40g, Fat: 8g, Fiber: 15g.

Japanese Miso and Tofu Stew

- **Preparation time:** 20 minutes
- **Ingredients:** 1 block silken tofu (cubed), 4 cups dashi stock, 3 tbsp miso paste, 1 cup seaweed (wakame), 1 green onion (sliced), 1 tsp sesame oil.
- **Servings:** 4
- **Cooking method:** Wok Cooking
- **Procedure:** 1. Heat dashi in wok, don't boil; 2. Dissolve miso paste in stock; 3. Add tofu, seaweed; 4. Warm gently, garnish with green onions and sesame oil.

- **Nutritional values:** Calories: 150, Protein: 10g, Carbohydrates: 10g, Fat: 8g, Fiber: 2g.

Fried Rice and Noodle Dishes

Classic Chicken Fried Rice

- **Preparation time:** 20 minutes
- **Ingredients:** 2 cups cooked rice, 1 lb chicken breast (cubed), 1 cup mixed vegetables (peas, carrots), 2 eggs (beaten), 2 tbsp soy sauce, 1 tbsp vegetable oil, 1 tsp sesame oil.
  - **Servings:** 4
- **Cooking method:** Wok Frying
- **Procedure:** 1. Heat oil, cook chicken until brown; 2. Add vegetables, stir-fry; 3. Push to side, scramble eggs; 4. Mix in rice, soy sauce, sesame oil.
- **Nutritional values:** Calories: 350, Protein: 25g, Carbohydrates: 40g, Fat: 10g, Fiber: 2g.

Spicy Shrimp Pad Thai

- **Preparation time:** 25 minutes
- **Ingredients:** 8 oz rice noodles, 1 lb shrimp (peeled), 2 eggs, 1 cup bean sprouts, 1/4 cup peanuts (crushed), 2 tbsp fish sauce, 1 tbsp tamarind paste, 1 tbsp brown sugar, 1 tsp chili flakes, 2 tbsp vegetable oil.
  - **Servings:** 4
- **Cooking method:** Wok Frying
- **Procedure:** 1. Soak noodles; 2. Stir-fry shrimp, set aside; 3. Scramble eggs; 4. Add noodles, fish sauce, tamarind, sugar, chili; 5. Mix shrimp, top with sprouts, peanuts.
- **Nutritional values:** Calories: 450, Protein: 30g, Carbohydrates: 60g, Fat: 12g, Fiber: 3g.

Vegetable Lo Mein

- **Preparation time:** 20 minutes
- **Ingredients:** 8 oz lo mein noodles, 2 cups mixed vegetables (broccoli, bell peppers, mushrooms), 2 tbsp soy sauce, 1 tbsp oyster sauce, 1 tsp ginger (minced), 2 garlic cloves (minced), 2 tbsp vegetable oil.
  - **Servings:** 4
- **Cooking method:** Wok Frying
- **Procedure:** 1. Cook noodles, set aside; 2. Stir-fry vegetables, garlic, ginger; 3. Add noodles, soy sauce, oyster sauce; 4. Toss until heated through.
- **Nutritional values:** Calories: 320, Protein: 8g, Carbohydrates: 55g, Fat: 8g, Fiber: 4g.

Beef Chow Fun

- **Preparation time:** 25 minutes
- **Ingredients:** 1 lb flank steak (sliced), 8 oz flat rice noodles, 1 onion (sliced), 1 bell pepper (sliced), 2 tbsp soy sauce, 1 tbsp hoisin sauce, 2 tsp sesame oil, 2 tbsp vegetable oil.
- **Servings:** 4
- **Cooking method:** Wok Frying
- **Procedure:** 1. Sauté beef, set aside; 2. Stir-fry onion, bell pepper; 3. Add noodles, beef, soy sauce, hoisin; 4. Drizzle with sesame oil, toss.
- **Nutritional values:** Calories: 400, Protein: 30g, Carbohydrates: 45g, Fat: 12g, Fiber: 3g.

Egg Fried Rice with Peas and Carrots

- **Preparation time:** 20 minutes
- **Ingredients:** 2 cups cooked rice, 1 cup peas and carrots (frozen), 3 eggs (beaten), 2 tbsp soy sauce, 1 tbsp sesame oil, 2 green onions (sliced), 1 tbsp vegetable oil.
- **Servings:** 4
- **Cooking method:** Wok Frying
- **Procedure:** 1. Scramble eggs in oil, set aside; 2. Stir-fry peas and carrots; 3. Add rice, soy sauce, sesame oil; 4. Mix in eggs, green onions.

- **Nutritional values:** Calories: 320, Protein: 12g, Carbohydrates: 45g, Fat: 10g, Fiber: 3g.

Spicy Tofu Stir-Fry Noodles

- **Preparation time:** 20 minutes
- **Ingredients:** 8 oz noodles, 1 lb firm tofu (cubed), 1 cup broccoli (florets), 1 red bell pepper (sliced), 2 tbsp chili sauce, 2 tbsp soy sauce, 1 tsp ginger (minced), 2 garlic cloves (minced), 2 tbsp vegetable oil.
- **Servings:** 4
- **Cooking method:** Wok Frying
- **Procedure:** 1. Fry tofu until golden; 2. Add vegetables, garlic, ginger; 3. Stir in noodles, chili sauce, soy sauce; 4. Toss until well mixed.
- **Nutritional values:** Calories: 380, Protein: 18g, Carbohydrates: 50g, Fat: 14g, Fiber: 4g.

Mushroom and Spinach Fried Rice

- **Preparation time:** 20 minutes
- **Ingredients:** 2 cups cooked rice, 2 cups spinach, 1 cup mushrooms (sliced), 2 eggs, 2 tbsp soy sauce, 1 tsp garlic (minced), 2 tbsp vegetable oil.
- **Servings:** 4
- **Cooking method:** Wok Frying

- **Procedure:** 1. Sauté mushrooms, garlic; 2. Add spinach, wilt; 3. Push to side, scramble eggs; 4. Stir in rice, soy sauce; 5. Combine all ingredients.
- **Nutritional values:** Calories: 300, Protein: 10g, Carbohydrates: 45g, Fat: 9g, Fiber: 2g.

Sweet and Sour Pineapple Fried Rice

- **Preparation time:** 25 minutes
- **Ingredients:** 2 cups cooked rice, 1 cup pineapple (cubed), 1 red bell pepper (chopped), 1/2 cup cashews, 2 tbsp sweet and sour sauce, 1 tbsp soy sauce, 2 green onions (sliced), 1 tbsp vegetable oil.
- **Servings:** 4
- **Cooking method:** Wok Frying
- **Procedure:** 1. Stir-fry bell pepper in oil; 2. Add pineapple, cashews; 3. Mix in rice, sauces; 4. Cook until heated; 5. Garnish with green onions.
- **Nutritional values:** Calories: 350, Protein: 8g, Carbohydrates: 55g, Fat: 12g, Fiber: 3g.

Wok Desserts

Wok-Fried Bananas with Honey and Nuts

- **Preparation time:** 15 minutes
- **Ingredients:** 4 ripe bananas (sliced), 2 tbsp honey, 1/4 cup mixed nuts (chopped), 1 tsp cinnamon, 2 tbsp butter.
- **Servings:** 4
- **Cooking method:** Wok Frying
- **Procedure:** 1. Melt butter in wok; 2. Add bananas, fry until golden; 3. Drizzle with honey; 4. Sprinkle nuts, cinnamon.

- **Nutritional values:** Calories: 200, Protein: 2g, Carbohydrates: 35g, Fat: 7g, Fiber: 4g.

Wok-Seared Pineapple with Brown Sugar Glaze

- **Preparation time:** 15 minutes
- **Ingredients:** 1 pineapple (sliced), 1/4 cup brown sugar, 1 tsp vanilla extract, 2 tbsp butter, Pinch of salt.
- **Servings:** 4
- **Cooking method:** Wok Frying
- **Procedure:** 1. Melt butter, sugar in wok; 2. Add pineapple, vanilla, salt; 3. Cook until caramelized.

- **Nutritional values:** Calories: 180, Protein: 1g, Carbohydrates: 30g, Fat: 7g, Fiber: 2g.

Chocolate and Nut Wok-Baked Brownies

- **Preparation time:** 25 minutes
- **Ingredients:** 1 cup all-purpose flour, 1/2 cup cocoa powder, 1 cup sugar, 2 eggs, 1/2 cup melted butter, 1/4 cup mixed nuts (chopped), 1 tsp baking powder.
- **Servings:** 4
- **Cooking method:** Wok Baking
- **Procedure:** 1. Mix flour, cocoa, sugar, baking powder; 2. Blend in eggs, butter; 3. Stir in nuts; 4. Pour into greased wok; 5. Cover, bake over low heat.
- **Nutritional values:** Calories: 350, Protein: 6g, Carbohydrates: 50g, Fat: 15g, Fiber: 3g.

Wok-Caramelized Apples with Cinnamon

- **Preparation time:** 15 minutes
- **Ingredients:** 4 apples (sliced), 1/4 cup sugar, 1 tsp cinnamon, 2 tbsp butter, 1/4 cup apple juice.
- **Servings:** 4
- **Cooking method:** Wok Frying

- **Procedure:** 1. Melt butter in wok; 2. Add apples, sugar, cinnamon; 3. Cook until soft; 4. Pour in juice, simmer.
- **Nutritional values:** Calories: 180, Protein: 1g, Carbohydrates: 35g, Fat: 5g, Fiber: 4g.

Wok-Fried Honey and Sesame Bananas

- **Preparation time:** 15 minutes
- **Ingredients:** 4 bananas (sliced), 3 tbsp honey, 2 tbsp sesame seeds, 2 tbsp butter.
- **Servings:** 4
- **Cooking method:** Wok Frying
- **Procedure:** 1. Melt butter in wok; 2. Add bananas, fry lightly; 3. Drizzle with honey; 4. Sprinkle sesame seeds.
- **Nutritional values:** Calories: 250, Protein: 2g, Carbohydrates: 40g, Fat: 10g, Fiber: 3g.

Wok-Baked Apple Crisp

- **Preparation time:** 25 minutes
- **Ingredients:** 4 apples (cubed), 1/2 cup oats, 1/4 cup flour, 1/4 cup brown sugar, 1/4 cup butter, 1 tsp cinnamon.
- **Servings:** 4
- **Cooking method:** Wok Baking

- **Procedure:** 1. Combine apples, cinnamon in wok; 2. Mix oats, flour, sugar, butter (crumbled); 3. Sprinkle over apples; 4. Cover, bake over low heat.
- **Nutritional values:** Calories: 300, Protein: 3g, Carbohydrates: 45g, Fat: 13g, Fiber: 5g.

Wok-Fried Mango with Coconut

- **Preparation time:** 15 minutes
- **Ingredients:** 2 mangoes (sliced), 1/4 cup shredded coconut, 1/4 cup brown sugar, 1 tsp lime zest, 2 tbsp butter.
- **Servings:** 4
- **Cooking method:** Wok Frying
- **Procedure:** 1. Melt butter, sugar in wok; 2. Add mangoes, lime zest; 3. Cook until caramelized; 4. Sprinkle coconut.

- **Nutritional values:** Calories: 220, Protein: 1g, Carbohydrates: 35g, Fat: 9g, Fiber: 3g.

Wok-Sizzled Berries with Vanilla Ice Cream

- **Preparation time:** 10 minutes
- **Ingredients:** 2 cups mixed berries, 1/4 cup sugar, 1 tsp lemon juice, Vanilla ice cream for serving.
- **Servings:** 4
- **Cooking method:** Wok Frying
- **Procedure:** 1. Heat berries, sugar, lemon juice in wok; 2. Cook until syrupy; 3. Serve warm over ice cream.
- **Nutritional values:** Calories: 150, Protein: 1g, Carbohydrates: 30g, Fat: 2g, Fiber: 3g.

Chapter VI: Regional Wok Wonders

Chinese Classics

Kung Pao Chicken

- **Preparation time:** 20 minutes
- **Ingredients:** 1 lb chicken (diced), 1/4 cup peanuts, 2 bell peppers (diced), 4 dried chilies, 2 tbsp soy sauce, 1 tbsp hoisin sauce, 1 tsp cornstarch, 2 garlic cloves (minced), 2 tsp ginger (minced), 2 tbsp vegetable oil.
- **Servings:** 4
- **Cooking method:** Wok Stir-Frying
- **Procedure:** 1. Heat oil, fry chilies, ginger, garlic; 2. Add chicken, cook through; 3. Toss in bell peppers, sauce mix; 4. Finish with peanuts.
- **Nutritional values:** Calories: 280, Protein: 26g, Carbohydrates: 10g, Fat: 16g, Fiber: 2g.

Mapo Tofu

- **Preparation time:** 25 minutes
- **Ingredients:** 1 lb silken tofu (cubed), 1/2 lb ground pork, 2 tbsp chili bean paste, 1 tbsp soy sauce, 1 tsp sugar, 1 tsp cornstarch, 2 garlic cloves (minced), 1 tbsp ginger (minced), 2 green onions (sliced), 2 tbsp vegetable oil.
- **Servings:** 4
- **Cooking method:** Wok Simmering
- **Procedure:** 1. Brown pork, ginger, garlic in oil; 2. Stir in bean paste, tofu, seasonings; 3. Simmer gently; 4. Thicken with cornstarch, garnish with green onions.
- **Nutritional values:** Calories: 300, Protein: 18g, Carbohydrates: 8g, Fat: 22g, Fiber: 1g.

Beef and Broccoli

- **Preparation time:** 20 minutes
- **Ingredients:** 1 lb flank steak (sliced), 2 cups broccoli (florets), 2 tbsp oyster sauce, 1 tbsp soy sauce, 1 tsp sugar, 1 tsp cornstarch, 2 garlic cloves (minced), 2 tbsp vegetable oil.
- **Servings:** 4
- **Cooking method:** Wok Stir-Frying
- **Procedure:** 1. Sear beef, set aside; 2. Stir-fry broccoli, garlic; 3. Combine beef, sauces, sugar; 4. Thicken with cornstarch.
- **Nutritional values:** Calories: 250, Protein: 26g, Carbohydrates: 12g, Fat: 10g, Fiber: 2g.

Egg Fried Rice

- **Preparation time:** 15 minutes
- **Ingredients:** 2 cups cooked rice, 4 eggs (beaten), 1 cup peas and carrots (diced), 2 tbsp soy sauce, 2 green onions (sliced), 2 tbsp vegetable oil.
- **Servings:** 4
- **Cooking method:** Wok Frying
- **Procedure:** 1. Scramble eggs, remove; 2. Stir-fry veggies; 3. Add rice, soy sauce; 4. Mix in eggs, green onions.
- **Nutritional values:** Calories: 320, Protein: 12g, Carbohydrates: 45g, Fat: 10g, Fiber: 3g.

Sweet and Sour Pork

- **Preparation time:** 25 minutes
- **Ingredients:** 1 lb pork (cubed), 1 bell pepper (cubed), 1 onion (cubed), 1/2 cup pineapple (cubed), 1/4 cup vinegar, 1/4 cup sugar, 2 tbsp ketchup, 1 tbsp soy sauce, 1 tsp cornstarch, 2 tbsp vegetable oil.

- **Servings:** 4
- **Cooking method:** Wok Frying
- **Procedure:** 1. Fry pork until golden; 2. Sauté veggies, pineapple; 3. Stir in vinegar, sugar, ketchup, soy sauce; 4. Thicken with cornstarch.
- **Nutritional values:** Calories: 330, Protein: 24g, Carbohydrates: 25g, Fat: 15g, Fiber: 1g.

Cantonese Steamed Fish

- **Preparation time:** 20 minutes
- **Ingredients:** 1 lb whole fish (cleaned), 2 green onions (sliced), 1 tbsp ginger (julienned), 2 tbsp soy sauce, 1 tsp sesame oil, 1 tsp sugar, Cilantro for garnish.
- **Servings:** 4
- **Cooking method:** Wok Steaming
- **Procedure:** 1. Place fish on plate, top with ginger; 2. Steam in wok until cooked; 3. Drizzle soy sauce, sesame oil, sugar; 4. Garnish with green onions, cilantro.
- **Nutritional values:** Calories: 200, Protein: 23g, Carbohydrates: 3g, Fat: 10g, Fiber: 0g.

Chinese Stir-Fried Noodles

- **Preparation time:** 20 minutes
- **Ingredients:** 8 oz chow mein noodles, 1 cup mixed vegetables (julienned), 2 tbsp soy sauce, 1 tbsp oyster sauce, 1 tsp sesame oil, 2 garlic cloves (minced), 2 tbsp vegetable oil.
- **Servings:** 4
- **Cooking method:** Wok Stir-Frying
- **Procedure:** 1. Cook noodles, set aside; 2. Stir-fry vegetables, garlic; 3. Add noodles, sauces; 4. Toss, finish with sesame oil.
- **Nutritional values:** Calories: 300, Protein: 8g, Carbohydrates: 50g, Fat: 8g, Fiber: 3g.

Szechuan Tofu and Green Beans

- **Preparation time:** 25 minutes
- **Ingredients:** 1 lb firm tofu (cubed), 2 cups green beans (trimmed), 2 tbsp chili paste, 1 tbsp soy sauce, 1 tsp sugar, 1 tsp ginger (minced), 2 garlic cloves (minced), 2 tbsp vegetable oil.
- **Servings:** 4
- **Cooking method:** Wok Stir-Frying
- **Procedure:** 1. Fry tofu until golden; 2. Sauté green beans, ginger, garlic; 3. Add tofu, chili paste, soy sauce, sugar; 4. Cook until beans are tender.

- **Nutritional values:** Calories: 220, Protein: 12g, Carbohydrates: 15g, Fat: 14g, Fiber: 4g.

Thai Treasures

Pad Thai

- **Preparation time:** 25 minutes
- **Ingredients:** 8 oz rice noodles, 1 lb shrimp (peeled), 2 eggs, 1 cup bean sprouts, 1/4 cup peanuts (crushed), 2 tbsp fish sauce, 1 tbsp tamarind paste, 1 tbsp brown sugar, 1 tsp chili flakes, 2 tbsp vegetable oil.
- **Servings:** 4
- **Cooking method:** Wok Stir-Frying
- **Procedure:** 1. Soak noodles; 2. Stir-fry shrimp, set aside; 3. Scramble eggs; 4. Add noodles, fish sauce, tamarind, sugar, chili; 5. Mix shrimp, top with sprouts, peanuts.
- **Nutritional values:** Calories: 450, Protein: 30g, Carbohydrates: 60g, Fat: 12g, Fiber: 3g.

Thai Basil Chicken

- **Preparation time:** 20 minutes
- **Ingredients:** 1 lb chicken breast (minced), 2 cups Thai basil leaves, 2 tbsp soy sauce, 1 tbsp fish sauce, 1 tsp sugar, 2 chili peppers (sliced), 3 garlic cloves (minced), 2 tbsp vegetable oil.
- **Servings:** 4
- **Cooking method:** Wok Stir-Frying
- **Procedure:** 1. Sauté garlic, chilies in oil; 2. Add chicken, cook through; 3. Stir in soy sauce, fish sauce, sugar; 4. Toss in basil leaves.
- **Nutritional values:** Calories: 300, Protein: 26g, Carbohydrates: 8g, Fat: 18g, Fiber: 1g.

Thai Green Curry with Vegetables

- **Preparation time:** 25 minutes
- **Ingredients:** 2 cups mixed vegetables (bell peppers, zucchini, peas), 1 can green curry paste, 1 can coconut milk, 1 tbsp fish sauce, 1 tsp sugar, 1 tbsp vegetable oil.
- **Servings:** 4
- **Cooking method:** Wok Simmering
- **Procedure:** 1. Sauté vegetables in oil; 2. Stir in curry paste; 3. Add coconut milk, fish sauce, sugar; 4. Simmer until vegetables are tender.
- **Nutritional values:** Calories: 300, Protein: 5g, Carbohydrates: 15g, Fat: 25g, Fiber: 4g.

Thai Pineapple Fried Rice

- **Preparation time:** 20 minutes
- **Ingredients:** 2 cups cooked rice, 1 cup pineapple (cubed), 1/2 cup cashews, 1 red bell pepper (chopped), 2 tbsp soy sauce, 1 tsp curry powder, 2 green onions (sliced), 2 tbsp vegetable oil.
- **Servings:** 4
- **Cooking method:** Wok Frying
- **Procedure:** 1. Stir-fry bell pepper in oil; 2. Add pineapple, cashews; 3. Mix in rice, soy sauce, curry powder; 4. Garnish with green onions.
- **Nutritional values:** Calories: 350, Protein: 8g, Carbohydrates: 55g, Fat: 12g, Fiber: 3g.

Thai Beef Salad

- **Preparation time:** 20 minutes
- **Ingredients:** 1 lb beef sirloin (sliced), 2 cups mixed salad greens, 1 cucumber (sliced), 1/4 cup mint leaves, 1/4 cup cilantro, 2 tbsp lime juice, 1 tbsp fish sauce, 1 tsp sugar, 1 chili pepper (sliced), 2 tbsp vegetable oil.
- **Servings:** 4
- **Cooking method:** Wok Searing
- **Procedure:** 1. Sear beef in wok, set aside; 2. Toss greens, cucumber, herbs; 3. Mix lime juice, fish sauce, sugar, chili; 4. Combine beef with salad, dressing.
- **Nutritional values:** Calories: 280, Protein: 26g, Carbohydrates: 8g, Fat: 16g, Fiber: 2g.

Thai Lemongrass Soup (Tom Yum)

- **Preparation time:** 30 minutes
- **Ingredients:** 4 cups chicken broth, 1 lb shrimp (peeled), 2 stalks lemongrass (minced), 1 inch galangal (sliced), 2 kaffir lime leaves, 2 chili peppers (sliced), 2 tbsp fish sauce, 1 tbsp lime juice, 1 tsp sugar, 1 cup mushrooms (sliced).
- **Servings:** 4
- **Cooking method:** Wok Simmering
- **Procedure:** 1. Boil broth with lemongrass, galangal, lime leaves; 2. Add shrimp, mushrooms, chili; 3. Season with fish sauce, lime juice, sugar.
- **Nutritional values:** Calories: 150, Protein: 20g, Carbohydrates: 8g, Fat: 5g, Fiber: 1g.

Thai Stir-Fried Noodles (Pad See Ew)

- **Preparation time:** 20 minutes
- **Ingredients:** 8 oz wide rice noodles, 1 lb chicken (sliced), 2 cups Chinese broccoli (chopped), 2 tbsp dark soy sauce, 1 tbsp oyster sauce, 1 tsp sugar, 2 eggs, 2 tbsp vegetable oil.
- **Servings:** 4
- **Cooking method:** Wok Stir-Frying
- **Procedure:** 1. Cook noodles; 2. Stir-fry chicken, set aside; 3. Add eggs, scramble; 4. Combine noodles, chicken, broccoli, sauces, sugar.
- **Nutritional values:** Calories: 420, Protein: 28g, Carbohydrates: 55g, Fat: 12g, Fiber: 3g.

Thai Spicy Eggplant with Basil

- **Preparation time:** 20 minutes
- **Ingredients:** 2 eggplants (cubed), 1 cup Thai basil leaves, 2 chili peppers (sliced), 2 garlic cloves (minced), 2 tbsp soy sauce, 1 tbsp fish sauce, 1 tsp sugar, 1 tbsp vegetable oil.
- **Servings:** 4
- **Cooking method:** Wok Stir-Frying
- **Procedure:** 1. Stir-fry eggplant in oil until soft; 2. Add garlic, chili; 3. Season with soy sauce, fish sauce, sugar; 4. Toss in basil before serving.
- **Nutritional values:** Calories: 150, Protein: 4g, Carbohydrates: 20g, Fat: 7g, Fiber: 6g.

Japanese Jewels

Chicken Teriyaki

- **Preparation time:** 20 minutes
- **Ingredients:** 1 lb chicken breast (sliced), 1/4 cup soy sauce, 2 tbsp mirin, 2 tbsp sake, 1 tbsp sugar, 1 tsp ginger (grated), 2 tbsp vegetable oil.
- **Servings:** 4
- **Cooking method:** Wok Frying
- **Procedure:** 1. Mix soy sauce, mirin, sake, sugar, ginger; 2. Sauté chicken in oil; 3. Pour sauce over chicken; 4. Cook until sauce thickens.
- **Nutritional values:** Calories: 280, Protein: 26g, Carbohydrates: 10g, Fat: 12g, Fiber: 0g.

Yakisoba (Japanese Stir-Fried Noodles)

- **Preparation time:** 20 minutes
- **Ingredients:** 8 oz soba noodles, 1 cup cabbage (shredded), 1 carrot (julienned), 1 onion (sliced), 1/4 cup yakisoba sauce, 2 tbsp vegetable oil, Pickled ginger for garnish.
- **Servings:** 4
- **Cooking method:** Wok Stir-Frying
- **Procedure:** 1. Cook noodles, set aside; 2. Stir-fry vegetables in oil; 3. Add noodles and sauce; 4. Toss together, garnish with pickled ginger.
- **Nutritional values:** Calories: 320, Protein: 8g, Carbohydrates: 55g, Fat: 8g, Fiber: 3g.

Miso Glazed Eggplant

- **Preparation time:** 20 minutes
- **Ingredients:** 2 eggplants (sliced), 2 tbsp miso paste, 1 tbsp mirin, 1 tbsp sake, 1 tsp sugar, 2 tbsp vegetable oil.
- **Servings:** 4
- **Cooking method:** Wok Frying
- **Procedure:** 1. Mix miso, mirin, sake, sugar; 2. Fry eggplant slices in oil; 3. Brush miso glaze over eggplant; 4. Cook until caramelized.

- **Nutritional values:** Calories: 180, Protein: 3g, Carbohydrates: 20g, Fat: 10g, Fiber: 6g.

Tempura Vegetables

- **Preparation time:** 30 minutes
- **Ingredients:** 2 cups assorted vegetables (bell peppers, mushrooms, sweet potatoes), 1 cup tempura batter mix, Cold water, Vegetable oil for frying, Tempura dipping sauce.
- **Servings:** 4
- **Cooking method:** Wok Frying
- **Procedure:** 1. Prepare tempura batter; 2. Dip vegetables in batter; 3. Fry in hot oil until golden; 4. Serve with dipping sauce.
- **Nutritional values:** Calories: 250, Protein: 4g, Carbohydrates: 35g, Fat: 10g, Fiber: 3g.

Japanese Style Garlic Fried Rice

- **Preparation time:** 15 minutes
- **Ingredients:** 2 cups cooked rice, 4 garlic cloves (minced), 2 eggs, 2 tbsp soy sauce, 2 green onions (sliced), 1 tbsp sesame oil, 2 tbsp vegetable oil.
- **Servings:** 4
- **Cooking method:** Wok Frying

- **Procedure:** 1. Scramble eggs in oil, set aside; 2. Sauté garlic; 3. Add rice, soy sauce; 4. Mix in eggs, green onions, sesame oil.
- **Nutritional values:** Calories: 320, Protein: 10g, Carbohydrates: 45g, Fat: 12g, Fiber: 2g.

Stir-Fried Shrimp with Wasabi Mayonnaise

- **Preparation time:** 20 minutes
- **Ingredients:** 1 lb shrimp (peeled), 2 tbsp mayonnaise, 1 tsp wasabi paste, 1 tsp soy sauce, 1 tsp lime juice, 2 tbsp vegetable oil.
- **Servings:** 4
- **Cooking method:** Wok Frying
- **Procedure:** 1. Fry shrimp in oil; 2. Mix mayonnaise, wasabi, soy sauce, lime juice; 3. Toss shrimp in wasabi mayo.
- **Nutritional values:** Calories: 280, Protein: 24g, Carbohydrates: 3g, Fat: 18g, Fiber: 0g.

Japanese Beef Stir-Fry

- **Preparation time:** 20 minutes
- **Ingredients:** 1 lb beef strips, 1 bell pepper (sliced), 1 onion (sliced), 1 tbsp soy sauce, 1 tbsp mirin, 1 tsp ginger (grated), 2 tbsp vegetable oil.
- **Servings:** 4
- **Cooking method:** Wok Stir-Frying
- **Procedure:** 1. Sauté beef, set aside; 2. Stir-fry onion, bell pepper; 3. Add beef, soy sauce, mirin, ginger; 4. Cook until combined.
- **Nutritional values:** Calories: 300, Protein: 26g, Carbohydrates: 10g, Fat: 16g, Fiber: 1g.

Japanese Spinach with Sesame (Spinach Gomae)

- **Preparation time:** 15 minutes
- **Ingredients:** 2 cups spinach (blanched), 2 tbsp sesame seeds (toasted), 1 tbsp soy sauce, 1 tbsp sugar, 1 tsp sesame oil.
- **Servings:** 4
- **Cooking method:** Wok Mixing
- **Procedure:** 1. Squeeze water from spinach; 2. Mix sesame seeds, soy sauce, sugar; 3. Toss spinach in sesame dressing; 4. Drizzle with sesame oil.
- **Nutritional values:** Calories: 100, Protein: 3g, Carbohydrates: 8g, Fat: 6g, Fiber: 2g.

Korean Kicks

Bibimbap (Mixed Rice with Vegetables)

- **Preparation time:** 30 minutes
- **Ingredients:** 2 cups cooked rice, 1 cup spinach, 1 carrot (julienned), 1 zucchini (julienned), 1/2 cup mushrooms (sliced), 1/2 cup bean sprouts, 1/4 cup gochujang (Korean chili paste), 4 eggs, 2 tbsp soy sauce, 2 tbsp sesame oil, 2 garlic cloves (minced), 2 tbsp vegetable oil.
- **Servings:** 4
- **Cooking method:** Wok Frying
- **Procedure:** 1. Sauté each vegetable separately, set aside; 2. Fry eggs; 3. In bowls, layer rice, vegetables, egg; 4. Top with gochujang, soy sauce, sesame oil.
- **Nutritional values:** Calories: 400, Protein: 12g, Carbohydrates: 55g, Fat: 15g, Fiber: 4g.

Japchae (Stir-Fried Glass Noodles)

- **Preparation time:** 25 minutes
- **Ingredients:** 8 oz glass noodles, 1 cup spinach, 1 carrot (julienned), 1 onion (sliced), 1/2 cup mushrooms (sliced), 2 tbsp soy sauce, 1 tbsp sugar, 1 tbsp sesame oil, 2 garlic cloves (minced), 2 tbsp vegetable oil.
- **Servings:** 4
- **Cooking method:** Wok Stir-Frying
- **Procedure:** 1. Cook noodles, set aside; 2. Stir-fry vegetables; 3. Add noodles, soy sauce, sugar, sesame oil; 4. Toss with garlic.
- **Nutritional values:** Calories: 320, Protein: 8g, Carbohydrates: 60g, Fat: 7g, Fiber: 3g.

Korean BBQ Beef (Bulgogi)

- **Preparation time:** 20 minutes (plus marinating time)
- **Ingredients:** 1 lb beef (thinly sliced), 1/4 cup soy sauce, 2 tbsp brown sugar, 1 tbsp sesame oil, 1 pear (grated), 2 garlic cloves (minced), 1 tsp ginger (minced), 1 onion (sliced), 1 carrot (julienned), 2 green onions (sliced), 2 tbsp vegetable oil.
- **Servings:** 4
- **Cooking method:** Wok Frying

- **Procedure:** 1. Marinate beef in soy sauce, sugar, sesame oil, pear, garlic, ginger; 2. Stir-fry beef, onion, carrot; 3. Garnish with green onions.
- **Nutritional values:** Calories: 350, Protein: 24g, Carbohydrates: 20g, Fat: 18g, Fiber: 2g.

Kimchi Fried Rice

- **Preparation time:** 15 minutes
- **Ingredients:** 2 cups cooked rice, 1 cup kimchi (chopped), 1/4 cup kimchi juice, 2 eggs, 2 green onions (sliced), 1 tbsp gochujang, 1 tsp sesame oil, 2 tbsp vegetable oil.
- **Servings:** 4
- **Cooking method:** Wok Frying
- **Procedure:** 1. Fry eggs, set aside; 2. Sauté kimchi in oil; 3. Add rice, kimchi juice, gochujang; 4. Stir in sesame oil, top with eggs, green onions.
- **Nutritional values:** Calories: 320, Protein: 10g, Carbohydrates: 45g, Fat: 12g, Fiber: 2g.

Tteokbokki (Spicy Stir-Fried Rice Cakes)

- **Preparation time:** 20 minutes

- **Ingredients:** 2 cups rice cakes, 1 cup fish cakes (sliced), 1/4 cup gochujang, 2 tbsp soy sauce, 1 tbsp sugar, 1 onion (sliced), 2 green onions (sliced), 2 cups water, 2 tbsp vegetable oil.
- **Servings:** 4
- **Cooking method:** Wok Stir-Frying
- **Procedure:** 1. Soak rice cakes; 2. Simmer gochujang, soy sauce, sugar, water; 3. Add rice cakes, fish cakes, onion; 4. Cook until sauce thickens, garnish with green onions.
- **Nutritional values:** Calories: 300, Protein: 10g, Carbohydrates: 50g, Fat: 7g, Fiber: 2g.

Sundubu Jjigae (Soft Tofu Stew)

- **Preparation time:** 25 minutes
- **Ingredients:** 1 lb soft tofu, 4 cups vegetable broth, 1 cup kimchi (chopped), 1/2 cup mushrooms (sliced), 1 onion (sliced), 2 tbsp gochugaru (Korean red pepper flakes), 1 tbsp soy sauce, 1 tbsp sesame oil, 1 egg, 2 garlic cloves (minced), 2 tbsp vegetable oil.
- **Servings:** 4
- **Cooking method:** Wok Simmering

- **Procedure:** 1. Sauté garlic, onion, mushrooms; 2. Add broth, kimchi, gochugaru, soy sauce; 3. Bring to boil, add tofu; 4. Simmer, finish with egg, sesame oil.
- **Nutritional values:** Calories: 200, Protein: 12g, Carbohydrates: 15g, Fat: 10g, Fiber: 3g.

Dakgangjeong (Sweet and Spicy Chicken)

- **Preparation time:** 30 minutes
- **Ingredients:** 1 lb chicken (cubed), 1/2 cup cornstarch, 1/4 cup soy sauce, 2 tbsp honey, 2 tbsp gochujang, 1 tbsp rice vinegar, 1 tsp garlic (minced), 1 tsp ginger (minced), 2 green onions (sliced), Vegetable oil for frying.
- **Servings:** 4
- **Cooking method:** Wok Frying
- **Procedure:** 1. Coat chicken in cornstarch, fry until golden; 2. Mix soy sauce, honey, gochujang, vinegar, garlic, ginger; 3. Toss chicken in sauce; 4. Garnish with green onions.
- **Nutritional values:** Calories: 380, Protein: 24g, Carbohydrates: 40g, Fat: 15g, Fiber: 1g.

Jeyuk Bokkeum (Spicy Pork Stir-Fry)

- **Preparation time:** 20 minutes (plus marinating time)
- **Ingredients:** 1 lb pork (thinly sliced), 1/4 cup gochujang, 2 tbsp soy sauce, 1 tbsp sugar, 1 tbsp sesame oil, 1 onion (sliced), 1 carrot (julienned), 1 green pepper (sliced), 2 green onions (sliced), 2 garlic cloves (minced), 2 tbsp vegetable oil.
- **Servings:** 4
- **Cooking method:** Wok Stir-Frying
- **Procedure:** 1. Marinate pork in gochujang, soy sauce, sugar, sesame oil, garlic; 2. Stir-fry pork, onion, carrot, pepper; 3. Garnish with green onions.
- **Nutritional values:** Calories: 320, Protein: 28g, Carbohydrates: 15g, Fat: 16g, Fiber: 2g.

Fusion Fantasies

Teriyaki Tacos

- **Preparation time:** 20 minutes
- **Ingredients:** 1 lb chicken (diced), 1/4 cup teriyaki sauce, 1/4 cup salsa, 1 avocado (sliced), 8 small tortillas, 2 tbsp vegetable oil.
  - **Servings:** 4
- **Cooking method:** Wok Frying
- **Procedure:** 1. Sauté chicken in oil; 2. Add teriyaki sauce; 3. Warm tortillas; 4. Assemble tacos with chicken, salsa, avocado.
- **Nutritional values:** Calories: 350, Protein: 25g, Carbohydrates: 30g, Fat: 15g, Fiber: 4g.

Thai Spiced Pasta

- **Preparation time:** 25 minutes
- **Ingredients:** 8 oz spaghetti, 1 cup coconut milk, 1 tbsp Thai red curry paste, 1 bell pepper (sliced), 1/2 cup peas, 1/4 cup basil leaves, 2 tbsp vegetable oil.
  - **Servings:** 4
- **Cooking method:** Wok Stir-Frying
- **Procedure:** 1. Cook pasta; 2. Sauté pepper, peas in oil; 3. Stir in coconut milk, curry paste; 4. Toss with pasta, basil.
- **Nutritional values:** Calories: 380, Protein: 10g, Carbohydrates: 55g, Fat: 15g, Fiber: 4g.

Szechuan-Style Pizza

- **Preparation time:** 30 minutes
- **Ingredients:** Pizza dough, 1/2 cup Szechuan sauce, 1 cup mozzarella cheese, 1/2 cup bell peppers (diced), 1/2 cup onion (diced), 1/4 cup peanuts (crushed), 2 tbsp vegetable oil.
  - **Servings:** 4
- **Cooking method:** Wok Baking
- **Procedure:** 1. Sauté peppers, onion in oil; 2. Spread Szechuan sauce on dough; 3. Top with cheese, veggies, peanuts; 4. Cook in wok-lid pizza setup.
- **Nutritional values:** Calories: 400, Protein: 15g, Carbohydrates: 45g, Fat: 20g, Fiber: 3g.

Mexican-Asian Beef Stir-Fry

- **Preparation time:** 20 minutes
- **Ingredients:** 1 lb beef strips, 1/4 cup soy sauce, 1 tbsp chili powder, 1 bell pepper (sliced), 1 onion (sliced), 1/4 cup cilantro (chopped), 2 tbsp vegetable oil.
- **Servings:** 4
- **Cooking method:** Wok Stir-Frying
- **Procedure:** 1. Marinate beef in soy sauce, chili powder; 2. Stir-fry beef, pepper, onion; 3. Garnish with cilantro.
- **Nutritional values:** Calories: 300, Protein: 26g, Carbohydrates: 10g, Fat: 16g, Fiber: 2g.

Indian-Chinese Chili Chicken

- **Preparation time:** 25 minutes
- **Ingredients:** 1 lb chicken (diced), 1/4 cup tomato sauce, 2 tbsp soy sauce, 1 tbsp garlic-ginger paste, 1 green chili (sliced), 1/2 cup onion (diced), 1/2 cup bell pepper (diced), 2 tbsp vegetable oil.
- **Servings:** 4
- **Cooking method:** Wok Stir-Frying
- **Procedure:** 1. Fry chicken in oil; 2. Add garlic-ginger paste, chili, vegetables; 3. Mix in tomato sauce, soy sauce; 4. Cook until sauce thickens.

- **Nutritional values:** Calories: 280, Protein: 25g, Carbohydrates: 10g, Fat: 14g, Fiber: 2g.

Korean-Italian Spicy Seafood Pasta

- **Preparation time:** 30 minutes
- **Ingredients:** 8 oz linguine, 1 lb mixed seafood, 1/4 cup gochujang, 1/4 cup cream, 1/4 cup Parmesan cheese, 2 green onions (sliced), 2 tbsp vegetable oil.
- **Servings:** 4
- **Cooking method:** Wok Stir-Frying
- **Procedure:** 1. Cook pasta; 2. Sauté seafood in oil; 3. Stir in gochujang, cream; 4. Toss with pasta, cheese, green onions.
- **Nutritional values:** Calories: 450, Protein: 30g, Carbohydrates: 45g, Fat: 18g, Fiber: 2g.

Cajun-Asian Shrimp and Grits

- **Preparation time:** 25 minutes
- **Ingredients:** 1 lb shrimp (peeled), 1 cup grits, 2 tbsp Cajun seasoning, 1/4 cup scallions (chopped), 1/4 cup soy sauce, 1/4 cup Parmesan cheese, 2 tbsp butter, 2 tbsp vegetable oil.
- **Servings:** 4
- **Cooking method:** Wok Frying

- **Procedure:** 1. Cook grits with butter, cheese; 2. Sauté shrimp in oil, Cajun seasoning; 3. Drizzle soy sauce over shrimp; 4. Serve shrimp on grits, garnish with scallions.
- **Nutritional values:** Calories: 400, Protein: 30g, Carbohydrates: 35g, Fat: 18g, Fiber: 2g.

Moroccan-Spiced Stir-Fry

- **Preparation time:** 20 minutes
- **Ingredients:** 1 lb lamb (sliced), 1 cup chickpeas, 1/2 cup raisins, 2 tsp Moroccan spice blend, 1/2 cup spinach, 1/4 cup almonds (slivered), 2 tbsp vegetable oil.
- **Servings:** 4
- **Cooking method:** Wok Stir-Frying
- **Procedure:** 1. Stir-fry lamb in oil, spice blend; 2. Add chickpeas, raisins; 3. Toss in spinach until wilted; 4. Garnish with almonds.
- **Nutritional values:** Calories: 350, Protein: 24g, Carbohydrates: 25g, Fat: 18g, Fiber: 5g.

Chapter VII: Meal Plans and Menus

Weeknight Dinner Plans

Quick Chicken and Broccoli Stir-Fry

- **Preparation time:** 20 minutes
- **Ingredients:** 1 lb chicken breast (sliced), 2 cups broccoli florets, 1/4 cup soy sauce, 2 tbsp honey, 1 tbsp garlic (minced), 2 tbsp vegetable oil.
- **Servings:** 4
- **Cooking method:** Wok Stir-Frying
- **Procedure:** 1. Sauté chicken in oil; 2. Add broccoli; 3. Stir in soy sauce, honey, garlic; 4. Cook until broccoli is tender.
- **Nutritional values:** Calories: 230, Protein: 26g, Carbohydrates: 15g, Fat: 8g, Fiber: 2g.

Beef and Pepper Fajitas

- **Preparation time:** 25 minutes
- **Ingredients:** 1 lb beef strips, 2 bell peppers (sliced), 1 onion (sliced), 1/4 cup fajita seasoning, 8 tortillas, 2 tbsp vegetable oil.
- **Servings:** 4
- **Cooking method:** Wok Frying
- **Procedure:** 1. Stir-fry beef in oil; 2. Add peppers, onion; 3. Sprinkle fajita seasoning; 4. Serve with warm tortillas.
- **Nutritional values:** Calories: 350, Protein: 25g, Carbohydrates: 30g, Fat: 15g, Fiber: 3g.

Shrimp and Asparagus

- **Preparation time:** 20 minutes
- **Ingredients:** 1 lb shrimp (peeled), 2 cups asparagus (chopped), 1 lemon (juiced), 2 garlic cloves (minced), 2 tbsp olive oil, Salt and pepper to taste.
- **Servings:** 4
- **Cooking method:** Wok Stir-Frying
- **Procedure:** 1. Sauté shrimp, asparagus in olive oil; 2. Add garlic, lemon juice; 3. Season with salt, pepper.
- **Nutritional values:** Calories: 200, Protein: 24g, Carbohydrates: 5g, Fat: 10g, Fiber: 2g.

Tofu and Vegetable Curry

- **Preparation time:** 30 minutes
- **Ingredients:** 1 lb tofu (cubed), 2 cups mixed vegetables (carrots, peas, bell peppers), 1 can coconut milk, 2 tbsp curry powder, 2 tbsp vegetable oil, Salt to taste.
- **Servings:** 4
- **Cooking method:** Wok Simmering
- **Procedure:** 1. Fry tofu in oil until golden; 2. Add vegetables, curry powder; 3. Pour in coconut milk; 4. Simmer until veggies are tender.
- **Nutritional values:** Calories: 350, Protein: 12g, Carbohydrates: 20g, Fat: 25g, Fiber: 4g.

Spicy Szechuan Noodles

- **Preparation time:** 20 minutes
- **Ingredients:** 8 oz noodles, 1/4 cup Szechuan sauce, 1/2 cup green onions (chopped), 1/4 cup peanuts (crushed), 2 tbsp sesame oil.
- **Servings:** 4
- **Cooking method:** Wok Tossing
- **Procedure:** 1. Cook noodles; 2. Toss in Szechuan sauce, sesame oil; 3. Garnish with green onions, peanuts.
- **Nutritional values:** Calories: 320, Protein: 8g, Carbohydrates: 45g, Fat: 12g, Fiber: 3g.

Lemon Garlic Tilapia Stir-Fry

- **Preparation time:** 20 minutes
- **Ingredients:** 1 lb tilapia (cut into pieces), 2 cups spinach, 1 lemon (juiced), 3 garlic cloves (minced), 2 tbsp olive oil, Salt and pepper to taste.
- **Servings:** 4
- **Cooking method:** Wok Stir-Frying
- **Procedure:** 1. Cook tilapia in olive oil; 2. Add garlic, lemon juice; 3. Stir in spinach; 4. Season with salt, pepper.
- **Nutritional values:** Calories: 210, Protein: 24g, Carbohydrates: 3g, Fat: 11g, Fiber: 1g.

Vegetable Fried Rice

- **Preparation time:** 25 minutes
- **Ingredients:** 2 cups cooked rice, 1 cup mixed vegetables (carrots, peas, corn), 2 eggs, 2 tbsp soy sauce, 1 tbsp sesame oil, 2 tbsp vegetable oil.
- **Servings:** 4
- **Cooking method:** Wok Frying
- **Procedure:** 1. Sauté vegetables in oil; 2. Stir in rice, eggs; 3. Add soy sauce, sesame oil; 4. Cook until eggs are set.
- **Nutritional values:** Calories: 320, Protein: 10g, Carbohydrates: 45g, Fat: 12g, Fiber: 2g.

Stir-Fried Pork and Snow Peas

- **Preparation time:** 20 minutes
- **Ingredients:** 1 lb pork (sliced), 2 cups snow peas, 1/4 cup hoisin sauce, 2 tbsp ginger (minced), 2 tbsp vegetable oil.
- **Servings:** 4
- **Cooking method:** Wok Stir-Frying
- **Procedure:** 1. Sauté pork in oil; 2. Add snow peas, ginger; 3. Stir in hoisin sauce; 4. Cook until peas are tender.
- **Nutritional values:** Calories: 300, Protein: 26g, Carbohydrates: 15g, Fat: 16g, Fiber: 2g.

Weekend Feast Ideas

Wok-Seared Steak and Vegetables

- **Preparation time:** 30 minutes
- **Ingredients:** 1 lb sirloin steak (sliced), 2 cups mixed vegetables (bell peppers, broccoli, carrots), 1/4 cup soy sauce, 2 tbsp oyster sauce, 1 tbsp garlic (minced), 2 tbsp vegetable oil.
- **Servings:** 4
- **Cooking method:** Wok Frying
- **Procedure:** 1. Sear steak slices in oil; 2. Remove steak, stir-fry vegetables; 3. Add steak, soy sauce, oyster sauce, garlic; 4. Cook until combined.
- **Nutritional values:** Calories: 320, Protein: 28g, Carbohydrates: 10g, Fat: 18g, Fiber: 3g.

Wok-Fried Lemon Herb Chicken

- **Preparation time:** 25 minutes
- **Ingredients:** 1 lb chicken thighs (cubed), 1 lemon (juiced and zested), 1 tbsp rosemary (chopped), 1 tbsp thyme (chopped), 1 garlic clove (minced), 2 tbsp olive oil.
- **Servings:** 4
- **Cooking method:** Wok Frying
- **Procedure:** 1. Marinate chicken in lemon, herbs, garlic; 2. Fry in olive oil until golden; 3. Serve with extra lemon zest.
- **Nutritional values:** Calories: 300, Protein: 23g, Carbohydrates: 3g, Fat: 22g, Fiber: 1g.

Spicy Wok Tofu with Cashews

- **Preparation time:** 20 minutes
- **Ingredients:** 1 lb tofu (cubed), 1 cup cashews, 1/4 cup chili sauce, 2 tbsp soy sauce, 1 bell pepper (diced), 2 tbsp sesame oil.
- **Servings:** 4
- **Cooking method:** Wok Stir-Frying
- **Procedure:** 1. Fry tofu in sesame oil; 2. Add cashews, bell pepper; 3. Glaze with chili sauce, soy sauce; 4. Serve hot.
- **Nutritional values:** Calories: 400, Protein: 18g, Carbohydrates: 20g, Fat: 28g, Fiber: 3g.

Wok-Baked Lobster with Garlic Butter

- **Preparation time:** 30 minutes
- **Ingredients:** 2 whole lobsters, 1/4 cup butter, 3 garlic cloves (minced), 1 lemon (juiced), 1 tbsp parsley (chopped), 2 tbsp olive oil.
- **Servings:** 4
- **Cooking method:** Wok Baking
- **Procedure:** 1. Split lobsters, brush with garlic butter; 2. Wok-bake with olive oil, lemon juice; 3. Garnish with parsley.
- **Nutritional values:** Calories: 400, Protein: 22g, Carbohydrates: 3g, Fat: 32g, Fiber: 0g.

Wok-Smoked Duck with Plum Sauce

- **Preparation time:** 40 minutes
- **Ingredients:** 1 whole duck (cut into pieces), 1 cup plum sauce, 1/4 cup hoisin sauce, 1 star anise, 2 tbsp ginger (minced), 2 tbsp vegetable oil.
- **Servings:** 4-6
- **Cooking method:** Wok Smoking
- **Procedure:** 1. Rub duck with hoisin, ginger; 2. Smoke in wok with star anise; 3. Glaze with plum sauce; 4. Serve with juices.
- **Nutritional values:** Calories: 500, Protein: 35g, Carbohydrates: 25g, Fat: 28g, Fiber: 1g.

Wok-Roasted Whole Fish with Asian Aromatics

- **Preparation time:** 35 minutes
- **Ingredients:** 1 whole fish (like snapper), 1/4 cup soy sauce, 1 tbsp ginger (sliced), 1/4 cup scallions (sliced), 1/4 cup cilantro, 2 tbsp sesame oil.
- **Servings:** 4
- **Cooking method:** Wok Roasting
- **Procedure:** 1. Score fish, stuff with ginger, scallions; 2. Drizzle with soy sauce, sesame oil; 3. Wok-roast till done; 4. Garnish with cilantro.

- **Nutritional values:** Calories: 300, Protein: 35g, Carbohydrates: 3g, Fat: 15g, Fiber: 1g.

Wok-Grilled Vegetables with Balsamic Glaze

- **Preparation time:** 20 minutes
- **Ingredients:** 2 cups mixed vegetables (zucchini, bell peppers, onions), 1/4 cup balsamic vinegar, 2 tbsp olive oil, Salt and pepper to taste, 1 tbsp rosemary (chopped).
- **Servings:** 4
- **Cooking method:** Wok Grilling
- **Procedure:** 1. Toss vegetables in oil, seasoning; 2. Grill in wok; 3. Drizzle with balsamic glaze; 4. Garnish with rosemary.
- **Nutritional values:** Calories: 120, Protein: 2g, Carbohydrates: 15g, Fat: 7g, Fiber: 3g.

Spicy Wok Paella

- **Preparation time:** 45 minutes
- **Ingredients:** 1 cup rice, 1 lb mixed seafood (shrimp, mussels), 1/2 lb chorizo (sliced), 1 bell pepper (diced), 1 onion (diced), 1/4 cup peas, 2 cups chicken broth, 1 tbsp paprika, Saffron threads, 2 tbsp olive oil.
- **Servings:** 4-6
- **Cooking method:** Wok Simmering
- **Procedure:** 1. Sauté chorizo, onion, pepper in oil; 2. Add rice, paprika, saffron; 3. Pour in broth; 4. Add seafood, peas; cook till rice is tender.
- **Nutritional values:** Calories: 450, Protein: 25g, Carbohydrates: 45g, Fat: 20g, Fiber: 3g.

Special Occasion Menus

Wok-Seared Scallops with Lemon Butter

- **Preparation time:** 20 minutes
- **Ingredients:** 1 lb sea scallops, 1/4 cup butter, 1 lemon (juiced), 2 garlic cloves (minced), 2 tbsp parsley (chopped), 2 tbsp olive oil.
- **Servings:** 4
- **Cooking method:** Wok Searing
- **Procedure:** 1. Sear scallops in olive oil; 2. Melt butter with garlic, lemon juice; 3. Drizzle over scallops; 4. Garnish with parsley.
- **Nutritional values:** Calories: 250, Protein: 20g, Carbohydrates: 3g, Fat: 18g, Fiber: 0g.

Crispy Duck with Plum Sauce

- **Preparation time:** 40 minutes
- **Ingredients:** 1 whole duck (quartered), 1 cup plum sauce, 1/4 cup soy sauce, 2 star anise, 2 tbsp ginger (minced), 2 tbsp vegetable oil.
- **Servings:** 4-6
- **Cooking method:** Wok Roasting
- **Procedure:** 1. Season duck with soy sauce, ginger; 2. Wok-roast with star anise; 3. Serve with plum sauce.
- **Nutritional values:** Calories: 560, Protein: 45g, Carbohydrates: 25g, Fat: 30g, Fiber: 1g.

Garlic and Herb Whole Roasted Fish

- **Preparation time:** 30 minutes
- **Ingredients:** 1 whole fish (like snapper), 1/4 cup mixed herbs (parsley, dill, basil), 4 garlic cloves (minced), 1 lemon (sliced), 2 tbsp olive oil.
- **Servings:** 4
- **Cooking method:** Wok Roasting
- **Procedure:** 1. Stuff fish with herbs, garlic, lemon; 2. Drizzle with olive oil; 3. Wok-roast until flaky.
- **Nutritional values:** Calories: 300, Protein: 40g, Carbohydrates: 5g, Fat: 15g, Fiber: 1g.

Wok-Fried Lobster with Ginger and Scallions

- **Preparation time:** 30 minutes
- **Ingredients:** 2 whole lobsters (split), 1/4 cup ginger (minced), 1/4 cup scallions (sliced), 1/4 cup soy sauce, 2 tbsp sesame oil, 2 tbsp vegetable oil.
- **Servings:** 4
- **Cooking method:** Wok Frying
- **Procedure:** 1. Fry lobster in oil; 2. Add ginger, scallions; 3. Drizzle with soy sauce, sesame oil.
- **Nutritional values:** Calories: 400, Protein: 28g, Carbohydrates: 5g, Fat: 30g, Fiber: 1g.

Spicy Wok-Seared Beef Tenderloin

- **Preparation time:** 25 minutes
- **Ingredients:** 1 lb beef tenderloin (sliced), 1/4 cup spicy marinade, 1 bell pepper (sliced), 1 onion (sliced), 2 tbsp cilantro (chopped), 2 tbsp vegetable oil.
- **Servings:** 4
- **Cooking method:** Wok Searing
- **Procedure:** 1. Marinate beef; 2. Sear in oil; 3. Add pepper, onion; 4. Garnish with cilantro.
- **Nutritional values:** Calories: 350, Protein: 30g, Carbohydrates: 10g, Fat: 20g, Fiber: 2g.

Wok-Charred Vegetables with Balsamic Reduction

- **Preparation time:** 20 minutes
- **Ingredients:** 3 cups mixed vegetables (asparagus, zucchini, bell peppers), 1/4 cup balsamic vinegar, 1/4 cup olive oil, Salt and pepper to taste.
- **Servings:** 4
- **Cooking method:** Wok Grilling
- **Procedure:** 1. Toss vegetables in oil, seasonings; 2. Wok-char till tender; 3. Drizzle with balsamic reduction.
- **Nutritional values:** Calories: 140, Protein: 3g, Carbohydrates: 15g, Fat: 8g, Fiber: 4g.

Wok-Smoked Whole Chicken with Aromatic Spices

- **Preparation time:** 60 minutes
- **Ingredients:** 1 whole chicken, 1/4 cup soy sauce, 2 tbsp five-spice powder, 1 star anise, 1 cinnamon stick, 2 tbsp honey, 2 tbsp vegetable oil.
- **Servings:** 4-6
- **Cooking method:** Wok Smoking
- **Procedure:** 1. Rub chicken with soy sauce, spices; 2. Wok-smoke with anise, cinnamon; 3. Glaze with honey.
- **Nutritional values:** Calories: 500, Protein: 40g, Carbohydrates: 10g, Fat: 30g, Fiber: 1g.

Deluxe Wok-Fried Rice with Seafood and Saffron

- **Preparation time:** 35 minutes
- **Ingredients:** 2 cups rice, 1 lb mixed seafood (shrimp, scallops), 1/4 cup peas, 1/4 cup carrots (diced), 1/4 teaspoon saffron threads, 2 tbsp olive oil.
- **Servings:** 4-6
- **Cooking method:** Wok Frying
- **Procedure:** 1. Cook rice with saffron; 2. Stir-fry seafood in oil; 3. Mix in rice, vegetables.
- **Nutritional values:** Calories: 400, Protein: 25g, Carbohydrates: 50g, Fat: 10g, Fiber: 2g.

Appendices

Common Wok Cooking Mistakes and How to Avoid Them

1. Overcrowding the Wok

One of the most common mistakes in wok cooking is overcrowding. This can lead to uneven cooking and steaming rather than stir-frying the ingredients, resulting in a lack of that coveted 'wok hei'—the essence of wok cooking. It's crucial to cook in batches if necessary. This approach ensures each ingredient gets enough attention and heat, preserving textures and flavors. For instance, when making a stir-fry, cook your protein first, set it aside, and then cook your vegetables. Combine everything at the end for a final toss. This technique not only enhances flavors but also maintains the distinct texture of each component.

2. Inadequate Preheating

Another error often encountered is insufficient preheating of the wok. A well-heated wok is essential for achieving the desired sear on ingredients, crucial in many Asian cuisines. The wok should be heated until it's nearly smoking. You can test the readiness by adding a few droplets of water. If they evaporate within seconds, your wok is ready. Remember, patience is key. Rushing this step can lead to undercooked or unevenly cooked meals that lack the depth of flavor you're aiming for.

3. Misjudging Oil and Temperature

The type and amount of oil used can greatly impact the outcome of your dish. Using the wrong oil, or not enough, can cause food to stick or not cook properly. It's important to use oils with a high smoke point, such as peanut or canola oil, to withstand the high temperatures required for wok cooking. Additionally, understanding the temperature needs of different ingredients is crucial. Delicate ingredients like garlic or green onions need a lower heat to avoid burning, while heartier vegetables and proteins can withstand higher heat.

In conclusion, mastering the wok is a journey of understanding its nuances and how it reacts with different ingredients and techniques. By avoiding these common mistakes, you're not just cooking; you're embarking on a culinary adventure that promises to be as rewarding as it is delicious. Remember, each step-in wok cooking is an opportunity to layer flavors and textures, creating dishes that not only satisfy the palate but also the soul. Happy wokking!

Index